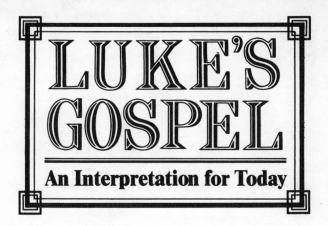

LUKE'S GOSPEL

An Interpretation for Today

ROBIN COOPER

Edward Arnold

A division of Hodder & Stoughton

LONDON   MELBOURNE   AUCKLAND

Acknowledgements

The publishers would like to thank Cambridge University Press for their permission to use the extracts from *The New English Bible* © 1970 Oxford and Cambridge University Presses.

© 1989 Robin Cooper

First published in Great Britain 1989

British Library Cataloguing in Publication Data

Cooper, Robin
  Luke's Gospel
  1. Bible N.T. Luke——Critical studies
  I. Title
  226'.406

ISBN 0–340–49227–9

Typeset in 11½ point Palatino by Photo·graphics, Honiton, Devon.
Printed and bound in Great Britain for Edward Arnold, the educational, academic and medical publishing division of Hodder and Stoughton Limited, Mill Road, Dunton Green, Sevenoaks, Kent, by Richard Clay Ltd., Bungay, Suffolk.

In Memory of the late Rt Rev Francis
Thomas STL, Bishop of Northampton, with
personal and grateful thanks.

Contents

Preface

This book, which presents a modern biblical approach to Luke's Gospel, is written for the classroom, with special reference for those studying for GCSE examinations. The book covers the whole of Luke's Gospel.

I have tried to encourage students to have an enquiring and critical approach to the Gospel and to ask themselves continually what relevance this Gospel has for today.

The book not only covers the text of the Gospel but also examines:

- the political and religious background to the time of Jesus;
- the purpose of the author and the characteristics of the Gospel;
- the influence of both the early Church and the author on the traditions about Jesus; and
- the continual interpretation of the Gospel for Christians today.

In each chapter concerning the text of the Gospel, there are work sections which follow the assessment objectives required by the various examination boards for GCSE: knowledge, understanding and evaluation. There are suggestions for practical work and questions for examination practice.

All biblical references are taken from the New English Bible. Quotations from Luke's Gospel may be identified by this logo

Sections which discuss Luke's Gospel 'for today' are in italics and are, therefore, easily identifiable throughout the book.

I would like to thank Lucie, my wife, for all her help in preparing the typescript and Nicole and Karen, my daughters, for putting up with me during the time of writing this book.

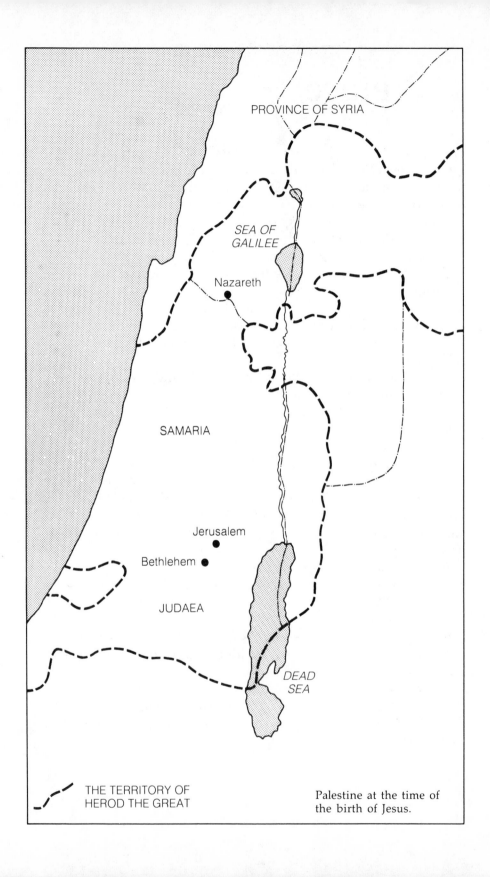

PROVINCE OF SYRIA

SEA OF GALILEE

Nazareth

SAMARIA

Jerusalem

Bethlehem

JUDAEA

DEAD SEA

THE TERRITORY OF HEROD THE GREAT

Palestine at the time of the birth of Jesus.

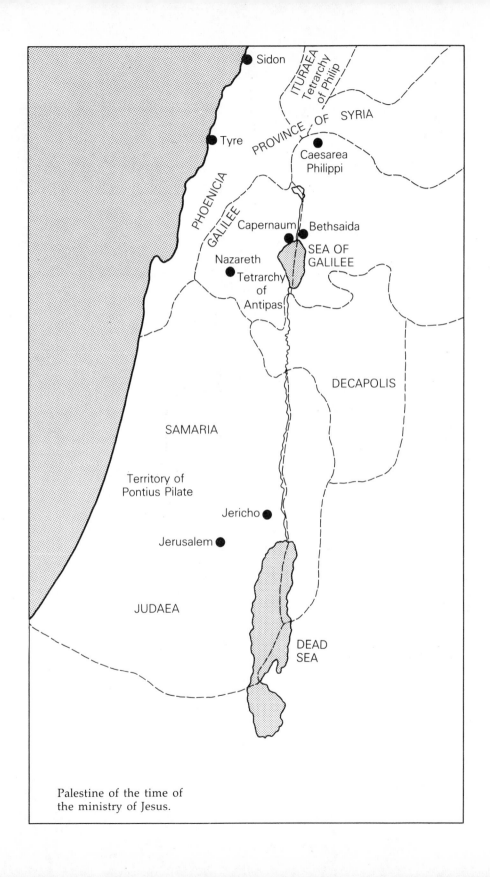

Palestine of the time of
the ministry of Jesus.

1 The Background to Luke's Gospel

The Political Background at the Time of Jesus

Herod the Great

For a hundred years or so before the birth of Jesus, Palestine had been under the rule of the Romans.

At the time when Jesus was born, Herod the Great was the 'puppet king' who ruled Palestine for the Romans. He served Rome well but because of this he received hostile opposition from some Jews, especially the Pharisees.

The main reasons for this opposition were:

1   Herod was not a Jew. He came from Idumaea, to the south of Judaea. He had no real claim to any royal throne and so he was regarded as a 'pretender', imposed on the Jewish nation by the Romans.
2   He showed little interest in Jewish law or customs. He provoked the Jews by promoting Greek culture and buildings in the holy city of Jerusalem.

Herod ruled from 37–4 BC. He was a clever man who brought an uneasy peace and stability to Palestine. He built new cities and was responsible for the building of the new Temple in Jerusalem.

Many people have condemned Herod as a cruel man and certainly he showed a cruel streak, especially towards his own family. His relationships were full of intrigue and conflict. He was passionately devoted to his second wife, Mariamne, but was equally capable of passionate jealousy. His mind was poisoned against her and her sons Aristobulus and Alexander. Convinced of her unfaithfulness, Herod had Mariamne executed in 29 BC and her sons, in 7 BC. In 4 BC Antipater, son of his first wife Doris, was also executed shortly before Herod's own death in the same year.

On the death of Herod the Great, the Roman Emperor Augustus divided the kingdom among three of Herod's sons, Archelaus, Herod Antipas and Philip. However, they were not given the title of 'king' like their father.

- Archelaus was appointed ethnarch (a title similar to 'governor') of Judaea and Samaria;
- Herod Antipas, tetrarch (a title for a ruler who was not considered important enough to have the rank of king; again it amounted to being a 'governor') of Galilee;
- Philip, tetrarch of the lands of Ituraea and Trachonitis which was to the north east of the Sea of Galilee.

Archelaus was deposed in AD 6 and sent into exile. The territory of Judaea and Samaria was placed in the hands of a Roman Procurator (a Roman officer with the rank of governor). The most well-known procurator of Judaea and Samaria was Pontius Pilate (AD 26–39).

Herod Antipas

Herod Antipas was the ruler responsible for the death of John the Baptist. He had him killed after John had criticised Herod's marriage to Herodias, the wife of his half-brother Herod Philip (Luke 3:19).

This was the same Herod that Pontius Pilate sent the accused Jesus to during his trial, on the excuse that, because Jesus was a Galilean, he came under the rule of the Tetrarch of Galilee (Luke 23:2–7).

SUMMARY

- During the days of Herod the Great and his successors, Palestine was a troubled province of the Roman empire. There was continual unrest.
- Most Jews hated the Romans, not only because they occupied the country by force but because they were also Gentiles (non-Jews).
- It was into this atmosphere that Jesus was born and grew up. In these troubled times Jesus conducted his ministry and was put to death.

The Religious Background at the Time of Jesus

The Sanhedrin

The Sanhedrin was the highest court of Jewish law. It dealt with all matters, both religious and political. The name 'Sanhedrin' means 'council'. The president of the council was the High Priest.

The origin of the Sanhedrin was the seventy men Moses appointed to assist him in judging the people of Israel. The seventy members of the Sanhedrin were drawn mainly from two opposing parties, the Sadducees and the Pharisees. In criminal cases the Sanhedrin could pass a sentence of death but could not carry out such a sentence without the approval of the Roman Procurator.

Pharisees

The Pharisees were far more influential among the people than the Sadducees. They were the progressive party of Judaism. For them religious life centred round the study and keeping of the Law of Moses. Their heritage can be traced back to the time of the destruction of the Temple in 586 BC, when the Jews were taken captive into exile by the Babylonians. All that the loyal Jew in exile had left to keep the faith alive was a strict keeping of the Law of Moses, contained in the Pentateuch. (The Pentateuch or the Torah is the Law of Moses found in the first five books of the Old Testament.)

In the second century BC, when Judah was occupied by the Greeks, the Pharisees were the ones who refused all Greek influences. They became known as the 'separated ones' (this is what the name Pharisee means) because of their refusal to compromise. Their aim was to keep alive the traditional Jewish faith.

WHAT THE PHARISEES BELIEVED

- The Pharisees wished to protect the Law and make it fit every need of daily life.
- They strictly kept the oral law, which was developed by the Scribes, to interpret the Law of Moses.

- In their desire to keep the Law, they surrounded it with:

  (a) a great many minute regulations;
  (b) volumes of explanations; and
  (c) all sorts of complicated additions.

- This 'oral law' was equally as binding as the written Law of Moses. It was later written down in two books called the *Mishnah* and the *Talmud*.
- The Pharisees looked forward to the coming of the Messiah.
- The Pharisees believed in a form of resurrection at the last day (the Day of Judgment).

Sadducees

The Sadducees claimed direct descent from Zadok who was the High Priest at the time of King Solomon (1 Kings 2:35). The Sadducees were priests. They were the upper class in Jewish society, living in ease and comfort. They had control of the Temple worship, sacrifices and finances. They were very conservative in their political outlook and wanted things to remain exactly as they were under the Romans. They were content, therefore, to work in co-operation with the Romans.

WHAT THE SADDUCEES BELIEVED

The beliefs of the Sadducees differed from other religious parties.

- They did not believe in the coming of the Messiah, especially the popular idea of the Messiah who would free the people from the Romans. This would lead to conflict with Rome and this must be avoided at all costs.
- Their only rule of religious, moral and social life was the **Law of Moses** as found in the first five books of the Old Testament (called the **Pentateuch** or the **Torah**). They took the Commandments of Moses literally.

- They laid little emphasis on the message of the prophets.
- They refused to be bound by the 'Oral Law' which explained the written Law of Moses (see Scribes and Pharisees).
- They did not believe in any form of resurrection.

Scribes

The Scribes belonged mainly, though not exclusively, to the party of the Pharisees. They were lawyers and sometimes are referred to as such in the Gospel.

The Scribes first appeared during the reign of Solomon. They became important in a world where few could write. Originally they were responsible for making accurate copies of the scriptures and for guarding the text against any errors. Slowly they became the legal authorities on the religious law, adding comments and interpretations of their own.

If parents wished their son to become a Scribe they took him to Jerusalem at the age of thirteen and enrolled him in one of the Rabbinical schools. His period of study lasted to the age of thirty when he became a Doctor of the Law.

The Temple

The Temple was central to Jewish belief. It symbolised the presence of God among the people.

The idea of the Temple went back to the time of Moses when God commanded a tabernacle (i.e. a tent) to be built in which to keep the Ark of the Covenant. The Ark was a portable shrine which accompanied the Israelites in their wanderings in the Sinai desert (Exodus 25 and 26).

The first Temple dates from the reign of King Solomon, c.970–930 BC and was built in Jerusalem. It was the centre of the religion. Only there could sacrificial worship take place (1 Kings 6).

This Temple was destroyed in 586 BC by the Babylonians. In 520 BC, on their return from exile, the Jews rebuilt the Temple.

A new and more splendid Temple was begun by Herod the Great in 20 BC. This was the Temple Jesus knew although it was not completed until after his death in AD 64. Six years later, in AD 70, this new Temple was destroyed by the Romans.

Herod's Temple was a magnificent building. It included the following features:

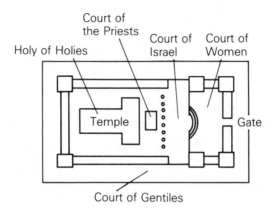

(a) **Court of the Gentiles**. This was a public place used as a market where traders sold the birds and animals used for sacrifices.

In this court could be found the money changers who changed the 'unclean' currencies such as Roman money into the sacred Temple money for the payment of Temple collections.

(b) **Court of Israel**. Only Jewish males were allowed in this court. Gentiles were forbidden to enter. There was a separate court for women. Again Gentiles were not allowed to enter.

(c) **Court of the Priests**. This was the most exclusive court. Only the priests were allowed to enter. In this area was the altar of sacrifice on which the birds and animals were killed.

(d) **Holy of Holies**. The Holy of Holies was the innermost shrine of the Temple. It was screened by a large veil or curtain. Behind it was the altar of incense.

The Holy of Holies was reserved for the presence of God. No one but the officiating priest was allowed to approach this most sacred place.

Temple Worship

The importance of the Temple worship, for the Jew of Jesus' day, can hardly be overestimated. The idea of sacrifice was central to this worship. There were three different types of sacrifice.

(a) **Morning and evening sacrifice**. Both took the form of the offering of incense; the sacrifice of a lamb without blemish; the meal offering of flour and oil, all of which was accompanied by prayer and praise.

(b) **Private offerings – daily**. Each day individuals would ask for private sacrifices to be offered to God in thanksgiving or forgiveness for sins.

(c) **Feast days**. On Feast days such as Passover, thousands of offerings were made.

All sacrifices were intended as a means of obtaining the forgiveness of God. The climax of the sacrificial year was the Day of Atonement when the High Priest entered the Holy of Holies and offered the blood of sacrifice as atonement for all the sins of Israel.

Once a year, at the Feast of Passover, vast numbers of Jewish pilgrims came to Jerusalem from all over to celebrate the Exodus. At this time the Temple resembled a huge slaughterhouse as thousands of lambs were sacrificed and handed to the people for the celebration of the Passover meal that night.

Temple worship ceased after the destruction of the Temple in AD 70. All that remains of Herod the Great's Temple is a course of huge stones where the Jews meet daily for prayer. This is called the Western Wall, popularly called the Wailing Wall because the Jews bewail the destruction of the Temple there.

The Synagogue

There was only one Temple but there was a synagogue in every Jewish community. The word 'synagogue' is a Greek word meaning 'assembly' or 'meeting' and represents the gathering of a congregation. As with the word 'church', the synagogue came to stand for the building as well as the people meeting there.

The origin of the synagogue goes back to the Babylonian period. The Jews were in exile after 586 BC and found themselves cut off from the Temple. They evolved a form of worship which required neither priest, Temple nor sacrifice. They gathered together to read the scriptures and to pray.

They found this to be so worthwhile that, on their return from exile, synagogue worship continued and became a major influence in religious life.

The synagogue was administered by a council of 'elders' who appointed a 'ruler' whose duty it was to prepare for the daily services and provide some general supervision. There were three services each day, at 9.00 am; 12.00 noon and 3.00 pm.

Synagogue worship is very important to the Jews. Since the destruction of the Temple in AD 70, it has been the synagogue that has kept the Jewish faith alive throughout the centuries even to the present day.

Understanding Luke's Gospel

The Formation of Gospel Tradition

In the earliest years of the Christian Church there was little need for a written record of the events of Jesus' life, death and resurrection. They had been observed by the disciples and passed on by word of mouth. That was sufficient because the early Christians expected Jesus to return immediately and set up the reign of God on earth (This event is called the Parousia).

As Christianity spread through the Roman Empire, so the stories of Jesus also spread. It is natural that some of these stories were developed and adapted to make the message of the Gospel relevant to people of differing backgrounds to the Jews.

In AD 66 the Jews rebelled against their Roman overlords in Palestine. This resulted in Jerusalem being destroyed in AD 70. James, the leader of the Jerusalem Church, was killed at this time. At about the same time, far away in Rome, Christians were being persecuted by the Emperor Nero. Thousands of Christians lost their lives. Amongst them, according to tradition, were St Peter and St Paul.

Jesus had not returned and the first generation Christians were beginning to die. Now the 'Gospel', the good news about Jesus, had to be preserved. The traditions about Jesus were collected and formed into books by the Evangelists. Of the many Gospels written, the Church, later on, chose four as being the ones that contained 'the faith'. These four were the ones named Matthew, Mark, Luke and John.

Oral Tradition

After the death and resurrection of Jesus, the stories about his life were passed on by word of mouth for some thirty years before the first Gospel was written. This is called the period of the 'oral tradition'.

The study of the oral tradition is called *form criticism*. Form criticism examines the way in which the traditions of Jesus were preserved and handed on in the time before the writing of the Gospels.

The form critics claim:
- The stories about Jesus can be categorised into four main 'forms'. These can be seen clearly in the Gospel narrative.
- The four forms are:

    (a) pronouncement stories (called paradigms). These are stories that lead to an important statement by Jesus. For example, the story of Jesus having dinner at Levi's house leads to Jesus telling the Pharisees, 'I have not come to invite virtuous people, but to call sinners to repentance' (5:32).
    (b) miracle stories: (all following a set pattern).
    (c) biographical sketches. These are stories that provide more detail about a specific person (see 19:1–10).
    (d) parables.

- The reason for the preserving and passing on of the traditions in this way was because they were used primarily by the early Church in its teaching of the community.
- The form critics claim that some development of the stories took place in the passing down of these traditions.
- Each story was separate and passed on in isolation with the possible exception of the story of the Passion.
- The context of each story in the Gospel was in the hands of the author himself.

When each Evangelist recorded the stories about Jesus he did so for a particular purpose. He did not write a biography. He wrote with a particular audience in mind and therefore, emphasised the points of interest most suited to that audience. The study of the author's influence on the oral tradition is called *redaction criticism*.

The redaction critics claim:

- It is important to realise that the Gospel writers were not writing history as we understand it
- They were not interested in the question 'What really happened?' They took for granted the historical events of Jesus; his birth; life; death and resurrection. The question they sought to answer was much more important. They asked continually, 'What does this mean for us?'. For example they would ask: 'What does it mean for Jesus to die on the Cross?', rather than 'What happened when Jesus was crucified?'
- It is inevitable that the Evangelist made changes to the traditions in his desire to say what the events of Jesus' life meant for his readers.

The Sources of Luke

The Gospels of Matthew, Mark and Luke are called the *Synoptic Gospels*. The word 'Synoptic' is a combination of two Greek words:

syn   = together
opsis   = view or sight

The word is used of the first three Gospels because they have a common outline of the story of Jesus and because they have much material in common.

A comparison of the three Gospels shows that they not only have a great deal in common but also, in many cases, the wording of individual stories is either identical or very similar (for example, compare Mark 2:3–12; Matthew 9:2–8; Luke 5:18–26).

Perhaps it is not very surprising to find the same stories in three books about the same person. What is surprising, however, is that such stories are told using the same, or very nearly the same, language. This must mean that there is a written connection between the three.

The question is, who wrote his Gospel first?

Source One
For a long time it was thought the order of the writing of the Gospels was Matthew, Mark, Luke. There are two main reasons, however, for believing this is not the order in which they were written.

1   Almost the whole of Mark's Gospel is found in Matthew or Luke or both.

(a)   95 per cent of Markan matter is found in Matthew.

(b)   65 per cent of Markan matter is found in Luke.

(c)   There are 622 verses in Mark of which 609 have parallels in Matthew and 357 have parallels in Luke.

(d)   There are only thirty-one verses belonging to Mark which do not appear in either Matthew or Luke or both.

2   Mark is the shortest Gospel. The 65 per cent of Markan material found in Luke is only one-third of Luke's Gospel. Two-thirds of Luke is not in Mark.

It is more likely for Matthew and Luke to add to Mark's material than for Mark to miss out material from the others. So the conclusion is that Mark's Gospel is one of the sources used by Luke.

Source One

One source of Luke is Mark's Gospel

Source Two

There are some 250 verses which are found in both Matthew and Luke but not in Mark. Again the wording of the stories is either identical or very similar (for example, compare Matthew 3:7–10; Luke 3:7–9). This close similarity indicates a second written source. It is not known what this source was. The letter 'Q' is used to represent the source (the first letter of the German word 'Quelle', meaning 'source').

'Q' is a collection of some of the teachings of Jesus, for example, The Temptations Luke 4:1–16/Matthew 4:1–11; The Centurion's Servant Luke 7:1–10/Matthew 8:5–10.

Source Two

A second source of Luke is 'Q'

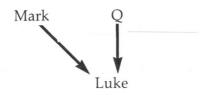

Source Three
There is also a lot of material that is only found in Luke's Gospel. This material is generally referred to as 'L'. It is doubtful if this existed in a written form and could well have been an oral source which Luke knew of and used. 'L' is a source which contains:

Miracles: the widow of Nain (7:11–17); the man with dropsy (14:1–6); the ten lepers (17:11–19); the crippled woman (13:10–17).

Parables: the good Samaritan (10:25·37); the lost son (15:11–22); the lost coin (15:8–10); the two debtors (7:41–42); the rich fool (12:16–21); the rich man and Lazarus (16:19–31); the Pharisee and the tax-collector (18:10–14); the fig tree (13:8–16); the friend at midnight (11:5–10); the unjust judge (18:1–8); the crafty steward (16:1–8).

Others: Certain other incidents regarding the Last Supper; the death and resurrection.

Source Three
A third source of Luke is 'L'

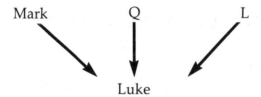

Source Four
Some scholars think that the infancy stories in Luke's Gospel come from a separate source. Certainly their atmosphere is different from the rest of the Gospel. They seem to have their origin in Judaism far more than the rest of the book. This source can be called 'I'.

Source Four
A fourth source of Luke is 'I'

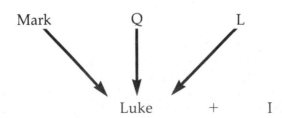

The Purpose of the Gospel

(**a**) By the time Luke wrote his Gospel the Romans had begun to persecute Christians. Luke's overall purpose is to try to show that the growing movement of Christianity is in no way dangerous to the state of Rome. It is, therefore, not surprising to find in Luke, that it is the Jews who are blamed for the death of Jesus. The Roman authorities are treated with a respect which is almost excusing them from any responsibility.

(**b**) It must not be forgotten that Luke is the author of two books in the New Testament; the Gospel and the Acts of the Apostles. In the Acts he shows how Christianity slowly spread, from the beginning on the day of Pentecost, into the Roman Empire. In the Gospel, Luke shows how Jesus moves towards Jerusalem in order for all this to take place through the death and resurrection of Jesus.

Luke's purpose can be expressed in a simple diagram.

Gospel	Jerusalem	Acts

The Characteristics of the Gospel

Certain other characteristics in the Gospel are used to support this main purpose of Luke.

Luke the historian
Even though Luke is not trying to answer the question, 'What happened?', he is at pains to set his account in a historical setting. He tries to fix dates at the key time of Jesus' birth and beginning of his ministry (2:1; 3:1).

Universalism
One major characteristic of the Gospel is its *universalism*. The Gospel is for all people, not just for the Jews (2:14; 2:32; 3:6; 4:16–30; 7:9; 9:52; 10:30–35; 17:12; 24:47).

Sympathy for the poor and sinners
The Gospel shows Jesus as a friend of outcasts, sinners and the poor (7:37; 14:15ff; 15:1ff; 19:1–10).

The importance given to women by Luke
In New Testament times women were largely uneducated, had no legal rights and no place in public life. In contrast to this, women play an important role in the Gospel. In the Infancy Narratives the role played by Mary and Elizabeth is a

major one (Luke 1:5–80; 2:1–52). In addition Luke records other stories involving women to a far greater extent than the other Gospels (7:11ff; 7:37ff; 8:1–2; 10:38–42; 21:1–4; 23:49–24:11).

The Emphasis on Prayer
Each of the Gospels mentions how Jesus went away into the hills to pray. Luke, however, has teaching on the subject of prayer that is not found in the other Gospels (11:5–10; 18:1–8; 18:9–14). He includes, also, examples of early Christian prayers (called Canticles) in his Infancy Narratives (1:46ff; 67ff; 2:14; 29ff).

The Gospel of the Holy Spirit
Luke has been called the *Gospel of the Holy Spirit*. His first two chapters are a record of the creative action of the Spirit (1:15; 1:35; 1:41; 1:67; 2:25–36). Jesus is guided by the Spirit (3:22; 4:1; 4:18; 10:21). At the moment of death Jesus hands back the Spirit to God (23:46). The Holy Spirit is promised to the disciples after the resurrection (24:49).

The Authorship of Luke's Gospel

(a) All historical evidence says that the Gospel was written by someone called Luke.

(b) One example of this early evidence can be found in the Muratorian Canon. (This is the earliest copy of the *Canon of Scripture*: The Canon of Scripture is the books of the Bible chosen to represent the faith of the Church). It contains this statement.

> 'The third Gospel according to Luke. After the Ascension of Christ, Luke, whom Paul had taken with him as an expert in the way (teaching), wrote under his own name and according to his own understanding. He had not, of course, seen the Lord in the flesh, and therefore, he begins to tell the story from the birth of John on.'

(c) Luke's superb Greek style and his emphasis on universalism lead many people to believe that he was of Gentile origin with Greek as his native language. He was, however, very knowledgeable in Jewish teaching and scripture.

(d) Luke was not an eye-witness, otherwise he would not have used Mark as a source. He says in the prologue to the Gospel that he was not a witness to the events themselves (1:1–4).

(e) Some scholars claim that Luke was a doctor. This is based on the comment by Paul in his letter to the Colossians where he writes, 'Greetings to you from our dear friend Luke, the doctor' (Colossians 4:14).

(f) Whoever the author was, he wrote two books. The Acts of the Apostles is written by the same hand. It may be that the two books were originally one manuscript.

(g) The author seems to have been a companion and friend of St Paul. A certain Luke is mentioned in his letters (2 Timothy 4:11; Philemon 24; Colossians 4:14).

(h) In the Acts of the Apostles there are three sections known as the 'we-passages'. These are passages where the author suddenly starts talking about what 'we did'. In the rest of the book he talks about what 'they did'. The obvious conclusion is that the writer himself was present on these occasions and has written some form of daily record or diary.

Conclusion
Luke had something to do with the writing of the two books. There are two alternatives:

1 Luke, companion of Paul wrote them both.
2 Luke wrote only the diary when he was with Paul on his journeys and that someone else wrote the books. The name Luke was given to the books.

The Date of Luke's Gospel

There are two possible dates:

An early date
The Acts of the Apostles ends with the imprisonment of St Paul in Rome awaiting trial. According to tradition, Paul was executed during the period of the persecution of the Christians in Rome around AD 65. This fact is not found in the Acts of the Apostles even though it would be a logical conclusion to the book. Could Luke have finished his Gospel before Paul's death? It is doubtful if this could be the case if

he used Mark as his main source as that Gospel was not written until about AD 65.

Some people seem to think that Luke wrote an early draft of his Gospel containing only the material from 'Q' and 'L' (this is called Proto-Luke). If this were so, then certainly this material could be as early as AD 60–65.

A later date

If Mark is the main source of the Gospel then the date of Luke must be later than his. It must be after AD 65–70. Luke's Gospel also contains references to the fall of Jerusalem which took place in AD 70 (21:20). So the completed Gospel is dated at around AD 75–80.

2 The Prologue and Birth Stories of Luke

The purpose of this chapter is to look at the prologue and infancy narratives of Luke. This can be done by examining:

– The prologue
– The structure of the birth stories
– The text of the birth stories

1 The announcement of the birth of John (1:5–25)
2 The announcement of the Birth of Jesus (1:26–38)
   The importance of the virgin birth for Christians today
3 The visitation (1:39–56)
4 The birth of John (1:57–80)
   Evaluation of chapter one
5 The birth of Jesus (2:1–20)
   Comment on the birth of Jesus
6 The circumcision and presentation of Jesus (2:21–40)
7 The boy Jesus in the Temple (2:41–52)

– *The importance of the birth of Jesus for Christians today*

The Prologue

Luke introduces his Gospel by giving both a brief summary of what had happened to the traditions of Jesus up to the time he writes. He also states his own purpose in writing a Gospel.
   He says that:

1 'many writers' had attempted to write accounts of the beginnings of Christianity;

2 the traditions about Jesus had been handed down by 'eyewitnesses' and 'servants of the Gospel';

3 he has himself followed the events closely; and

4 he has decided to write a 'connected narrative' so that it can be seen that the teaching of Christianity is well-founded and true. (Luke 1:1–4)

It is important to understand the nature of the claims that Luke is making.

He is not saying his Gospel is based on eye-witness accounts of the life and ministry of Jesus, in the sense of recording the recollections of one or more of the apostles or disciples.

He points out quite clearly that the content of the Gospel is based on tradition 'handed down to us'. In other words, it is more realistic to say that it contains the oral stories and traditions which had been passed down by the members of the early Church. This 'oral tradition' was open to all the influence and development of the earliest Church (see chapter 1).

When Luke claims to be writing a 'connected narrative' of 'authentic knowledge', it does not mean that he is writing biography in the sense of accurate newspaper reporting. He is concerned to show the meaning of the events he is describing. He is not answering the question 'What happened?' but 'What does this event mean?' (see chapter 1).

Luke dedicates the book to Theophilus. This Greek name means 'beloved of God'. It may or may not be the actual name of a person to whom the book is dedicated.

It has been suggested that 'Theophilus' was not the name of a person at all but stood for all Christians, that is, those 'beloved of God'.

What is more likely is that Theophilus was a person who held official rank within the Roman empire for his title is 'Excellency'. The use of this title suggests that his 'Excellency' was not a Christian, otherwise he would have been addressed as 'brother'.

In all probability he was some high-ranking officer of the empire who was interested in the new faith of Christianity.

The Structure of the Birth Stories

Luke records the announcement and birth of two babies; John the Baptist and Jesus. Both stories follow the same dramatic format. He uses the Old Testament as a basis on which to build what he wants to say about the births of these two babies.

A comparison of the two stories shows how Luke has used the same structure in each.

THE ANNOUNCEMENTS OF THE BIRTHS

John the Baptist (1:5–25)	Jesus (1:26–38)
(a) The parents are introduced; no child expected (barren) (1:5–10)	The parents are introduced; no child expected (unmarried) (1:26–27)
(b) appearance of the Angel (1:11)	appearance of the Angel (1:28)
(c) anxiety of Zechariah (1:12)	anxiety of Mary (1:29)
(d) do not be afraid (1:13)	do not be afraid (1:30)
(e) your wife will bear a son (1:13)	you will bear a son (1:31)
(f) you shall name him John (1:13)	you shall name him Jesus (1:31)
(g) he will be great (1:15)	he will be great (1:32)
(h) how can I be sure of this? (1:18)	how can this be? (1:34)
(i) I have been sent to . . . speak to you (1:19)	The Holy Spirit will come upon you (1:35)
(j) Sign given: dumbness (1:20)	Sign given: Elizabeth has conceived (1:36)
(k) Zechariah is silent (1:22)	Mary accepts her calling (1:38)
(l) Zechariah went home (1:23)	The Angel went away (1:38)

THE BIRTHS OF JOHN AND JESUS

(a) The birth of John (1:57–58)	The birth of Jesus (2:1–12) Canticle of the Angels ('Canticle' is a sacred song) (2:13–14)
(b) Joy at the birth (1:58)	Joy at the birth (2:15–18)
(c) John circumcised and named (1:59–64)	Jesus circumcised and named (2:21)

(d) reaction of neighbours (1:65–66)	reaction of Simeon and Anna (2:25–38)
(e) Canticle: Benedictus (1:68–79)	Canticle: Nunc Dimittis (2:29–32)
(f) Refrain: The child grew . . . (1:80)	Refrain: the child grew . . . (2:40)

How far is Luke writing History?
Luke skilfully sets his accounts in a historical setting with the use of names, geographical places and times within the historical period.

It should not be forgotten, however, that Luke's main purpose is to say what it means for John the Baptist and Jesus to be born. He wishes to put over the certainty that salvation through the Christ-figure, which was promised in the Old Testament, is about to take place.

The birth stories contain legend and poetry as well as their historical setting. This does not mean that they are not true. It means that their truth is symbolic. In legend and poetry, truth is not to be found in the literal interpretation of the words but in the image they portray. The birth stories of Luke must be interpreted in this way.

The Text of the Birth Stories

The Announcement of the Birth of John (1:5–25)

Luke sets his birth stories in the reign of Herod the Great. He introduces, immediately, the future parents of John.

Father: Zechariah, (a name which means 'God has remembered') was a priest who belonged to the Abijah section of the priesthood. This was the eighth of twenty-four divisions in which the priests were listed. These divisions took their names from the twenty-four grandsons of the first High Priest, Aaron, the brother of Moses. Each division took it in turn to serve in the Temple in Jerusalem.

Mother: Zechariah's wife was called Elizabeth (a name which means 'God will protect us'). Elizabeth was barren, which means that she was unable to have children. In those days this was looked upon, by some, as a punishment from God. Elizabeth was now past the child-bearing age.

It was the turn of the eight hundred priests of the division of Abijah to serve in the Temple. As there were so many, the duties were given out by casting lots (a practice similar to tossing a coin or drawing straws). The greatest privilege was to be chosen to burn incense in front of the tabernacle of the Lord in the Temple (see chart of Temple, p. 6).

The incense symbolised the offering of the praise of the whole nation to God. The priest would then emerge from the Holy of Holies and give God's blessing to the people.

Zechariah was chosen for this task. While he was in the sanctuary the angel Gabriel appeared to him. This story is similar to the experience of Daniel in the Old Testament. He also received a message from Gabriel. He was afraid and was told not to fear. He was struck dumb too and later had his speech returned (Daniel 10).

In Zechariah's case the angel's message was that his wife Elizabeth was to have a child and he must be called John, a name which means 'God is gracious'.

The poetry of this passage is based on Old Testament passages. Luke weaves them together into a masterpiece of poetry.

The message can be summarised (Old Testament parallel passages are given):

1   the child will be called John (see Genesis 17:19; Judges 13:4–5);
2   he will drink no wine or strong drink. This was part of the Nazarite vow which a person took if they were dedicating their life to God. (Numbers 6:2–3; Judges 13:14)
3   from the moment of birth he will be consecrated to God by the gift of the Holy Spirit. (Jeremiah 1:5)
4   John is cast in the figure of Elijah who, according to Jewish belief, would return to prepare the way for the Messiah. (Malachi 3:1–4:5)

This story ends with Zechariah unable to pronounce the
blessing on the people because of his dumbness. He returned
home to Elizabeth and in time she conceived. She kept
herself to herself for five months, content in the knowledge
that those who had gossiped about her because she had no
children, would now be silenced.

The Announcement of the Birth of Jesus (1:26–38)

When Elizabeth was six months pregnant, Gabriel appeared
again. This time he was sent to Mary who lived in Nazareth,
a little town in Galilee. Mary was engaged to Joseph, who
came from Bethlehem, the house of David, near Jerusalem, in
Judaea.

Mary was a virgin. Luke is most anxious to make this clear
and he uses the Greek word 'parthenos' twice in the opening
sentence. 'Parthenos' means 'virgin' in the sexual sense of the
word. This word is sometimes translated as 'girl' (1:26–38).

The opening words of the angel form the beginning of the
prayer called the 'Hail Mary'. The words can be translated,
'Hail (Mary) full of grace, the Lord is with you' (1:28). Some
later copies of Luke include, at this point, the second line of
the 'Hail Mary'; 'Blessed are you among women'.

The angel went on to tell Mary that she would have a
child. The same format is used as in the case of the
announcement of the birth of John. This time, however, the
content is much more Messianic in flavour. All the hopes and
thoughts of the Messiah are summed up in the words of
Gabriel.

1 The child will be called Jesus, a name which means 'God
   is salvation'.
2 He is described as 'great'. This adjective is normally
   reserved for God in the Old Testament.
3 His title will be 'Son of the Most High'. This term is an
   alternative for 'Son of God'.
4 Like his ancestor, King David, he will rule over Israel but
   his reign will be for ever. These words are similar to
   those used of the Messianic figure in the writings of the
   prophet Isaiah (Isaiah 9:5–7).

Mary obviously understood the message of the angel to mean
that she would conceive a child immediately, for she pointed
out that she was an unmarried woman.

The angel's answer is the foundation of the teaching about the virgin birth. Her conception was to be brought about by the creative power of God and as a result of this the child would be called 'Son of God'. These words indicate clearly the virginal conception of Jesus.

Mary accepted the message of the angel with complete trust and obedience. She was prepared to trust God and the story closes with the simple words of acceptance. 'I am the Lord's servant; as you have spoken, so be it' (1:38).

The importance of the virgin birth for Christians today

Even though the credal statements of the universal Church include the phrase that Jesus was 'born of the Virgin Mary', Christians are divided on the interpretation of this event. Some would consider the story to be historically important; while others would see its importance only in terms of the developing faith of the Church.

Those taking the former view would claim:
- *it is important that the birth of Jesus was unique. They would say that this is the only fitting way for the Son of God to be born;*
- *both Matthew and Luke have recorded the event in historical terms;*
- *the event was prophesied in the Old Testament;*
- *it cannot be proved that the virgin birth did not happen.*

Those taking the latter view would claim:
- *there is no knowledge of the idea of the virgin birth before the Gospels were written;*
- *the story was constructed to 'fulfil' the Old Testament prophecies;*
- *the stories illustrate the Church's understanding of who Jesus was;*
- *it cannot be proved the virgin birth happened.*

The Visitation (1:39–56)

Mary went to visit Elizabeth. As she greeted her, the unborn child in Elizabeth's womb 'leapt for joy'. This idea of harmony between the two unborn children is not borne out in the rest of the Gospel. Later on, John even doubted the fact that Jesus was the Messiah, sending two of his own disciples to ask Jesus the question, 'Are you the one who is to come, or are we to expect some other?' (7:18–19).

Elizabeth uses the title 'my Lord' of Jesus. It is doubtful if Elizabeth would have given this title to the unborn Jesus as it was first used as a title of adoration after the resurrection. Jesus is never called 'Lord' in the earliest Gospel of Mark, whereas Luke, looking back, refers to Jesus as 'Lord' throughout his Gospel.

In reply to Elizabeth's greeting, Mary proclaims the Magnificat. This is an early Christian song called a *canticle*. In it, all the pure hope of the belief of the Jews in the Messiah can be found. It is a song of praise.

It is not known who the author of the Magnificat was. Some would say it is Mary herself. Others, that it was the work of Luke himself or was already part of the source from which the birth stories come. Whoever the author was, the Magnificat is a complex piece of poetry.

The canticle is based on the song of Hannah (Samuel's mother) found in the Old Testament (1 Samuel 2:1–10). There are other Old Testament influences, all of which join together in making the song a poem of praise to God.

The message of the Magnificat can be summarised:

1:48–50 The Servant:
- Having already taken on the role of the servant, Mary develops this thought further. The great God has favoured his lowly servant and from now on she will be called 'blessed'. The mercy shown to her is available to all who respond to him. God cares for them.

1:51–53 God's relationship with people:
- The second part of the canticle shows the truth of the never changing relationship between God and people. It is, and always will be, those who know their need of God who receive his help. Those who consider themselves to be self-sufficient have no awareness of God or their need of him.

1:54–55 God's Promise:
- The final sentence of the canticle expresses the hope of Israel. God has come to Israel's help. The promises

> made in Old Testament times are about to come true.
> The inference is that the Messiah is about to be born.

Luke records that Mary stayed with Elizabeth for three
months so it is possible that she was still with her when
John was born.

The Birth of John (1:57–80)

When John was born there was great joy among the family.
On the eighth day the child was circumcised according to the
Jewish law. This was the sign of admission into the people of
God. It was at this ceremony that the child was given his
name. Luke explains how the child came to be called John
and not, as was the custom, Zechariah after his father. At the
moment of the naming of the child, Zechariah's speech
returned and his first act, inspired by the Holy Spirit, was to
praise God. The words Zechariah used are called 'The
Benedictus'.

The Benedictus falls into two parts. The first part (1:68–75)
is distinctly Jewish in flavour and is similar to prayers used
at the time of circumcision. The second part (1:76–79) is more
obviously Christian and contains a summary of the part John
the Baptist was to play in preparing the way for Jesus the
Christ.

This change of theme in v.76 has led some scholars to
suggest that the second part is an addition inserted into the
narrative. If this is so, then the author of part two is just as
clever, for the Benedictus is also full of poetry based on the
Old Testament.

The message of the Benedictus can be summarised:

Part 1 (1:67–75)
- The canticle begins with the phrase found many
  times in the Psalms. 'Praise to the God of Israel'
  (Psalm 41:13).
- God is praised for directly intervening in the affairs
  of his people and giving them a 'deliverer'. The
  salvation would come through the proper course, the

House of David. This salvation had been spoken of many times by all the prophets. It was a salvation promised by God, through the covenant (an agreement) with Abraham, and had been constantly renewed throughout Jewish history.

Part 2 (1:76–78)
- The little child is to become the Elijah figure, mentioned in the prophecies of Malachi and Isaiah, who would prepare the way.
- Christians read into the verses that Zechariah is saying that John will prepare for the coming of the Christ. God will save his people from their sins with mercy and forgiveness. He will 'give light to the people who walk in darkness and live in a land of deep shadow' (Isaiah 9:2). He will do this by bringing 'the morning sun from heaven' (1:78). This is a rare title for the Christ.

The story of John's birth is brought to a close by the use of the sentence. 'As the child grew up he became strong in spirit' (1:80). Luke uses this phrase on two more occasions to draw to a close stories concerning the infant and the boy Jesus (2:40; 2:52).

EVALUATION OF CHAPTER ONE

- There can be little doubt of the author's skill in this opening chapter. The masterly use of the Old Testament only adds to its beauty.
- It is this dependence on the Old Testament, however, that makes it difficult to think that Luke is writing factual history. It seems that legend plays a large part in this chapter and it is virtually impossible to see the dividing line between legend and history.
- The purpose of the author is to comment on who John and Jesus are.

The Birth of Jesus (Luke 2:1–20)

As with the birth of John, Luke tries to set the birth of Jesus in the context of world history. In so doing he creates a problem that has not yet been solved. Luke claims that Caesar Augustus ordered a census to be taken but there is no record of a census happening at that time.

It is possible to arrive at a probable date for the birth of Jesus by careful investigations.

- Caesar Augustus ruled from 30 BC–AD 14. He ordered a census throughout the 'Roman world'. This is probably an exaggeration. It does, however, give us the broad dates within which Jesus was born.
- It is known from Egyptian history that from AD 20 a census of householders took place every fourteen years.
- It is also known that a similar census took place in Syria in AD 6. Palestine fell within the area covered by the Syrian census.
- If, therefore, the fourteen year rule applied to Syria as well as Egypt, then there may have been a previous census in 8 BC, a date that is not too early for the birth of Jesus.
- Luke claims that Quirinius was Governor of Syria and Josephus, the Jewish historian, claims that Quirinius carried out the Syrian census in AD 6.
- AD 6 is too late for the birth of Jesus, as it is well-known that Jesus was born in the reign of Herod the Great. Herod died in 4 BC. Luke is wrong in saying that the census carried out at the birth of Jesus was done in the time of Quirinius.
- Between 10–7 BC, however, Quirinius was known to be on military service in the Syrian area and therefore there is the possibility of him being involved in a previous census even though he was not the governor at the time.
- In spite of all this, the actual year of the birth of Jesus is unknown, although it was probably between 8–6 BC.

Luke states that everyone went to his own town to be registered. This was possible. Such journeys are to be found in Egyptian writings of this period. Joseph and Mary went to Bethlehem, the royal city of David, because Joseph belonged to that family.

Mary gave birth to Jesus in a Bethlehem outhouse and used a manger for a crib. At the moment of birth Luke says that the Angel of the Lord appeared to some shepherds with the message of the birth. He was accompanied by

> a great company of the heavenly host, singing the praises of God (2:13).

The shepherds hurried to Bethlehem to see for themselves and found it to be as they had been told. They spread the joyful news throughout the neighbourhood. Mary

> treasured up all these things and pondered over them (2:19).

Comment on the Birth of Jesus

- Although the style of writing has changed in this second chapter and it seems, because of its historical setting, to be more like history, the question of whether Luke is writing history must still be asked.
- Luke seems to be continuing his earlier practice of combining symbolism and Old Testament overtones with basic historical facts.
- The story of Jesus' birth seems to be an expansion of an Old Testament prophecy found in Micah.

> 'But you, Bethlehem . . .
> small as you are to be among Judah's clans,
> out of you shall come forth a governor for Israel,
> one whose roots are far back in the past,
> in days gone by.
> Therefore only so long as a woman is in labour
> shall he give up Israel;
> and then those that survive of his race
> shall rejoin their brethren.
> He shall appear and be their shepherd
> in the strength of the Lord,
> in the majesty of the name of the Lord his God.
> And they shall continue,
> for now his greatness shall reach to the ends of the earth;
> and he shall be a man of peace' (Micah 5:2–5).

- The message about Jesus' birth is given to the shepherds. It is traditional to see the shepherds as the poor. While it is certainly in keeping with the character of Luke's Gospel to present the message of Jesus to the poor first of all, it should also be noted that the symbolism does not stop at this point. There is a second meaning to be found in the character of the shepherds. The first leaders of Israel, Abraham, Isaac and Jacob were shepherds; so was Moses and not least, King David. Even God is called the 'Shepherd of Israel' (Psalm 23:1). So there is a royal significance present in the announcement of the birth of Jesus by the Angel.
- The message of the Angel contains three titles of great importance given to Jesus (see Chapter 9).

   - *Deliverer* (that is – Saviour). This is a title only used by Luke. Salvation is one of the main themes of the Gospel.
   - *Christ.* Jesus is the anointed one of God. He is the one who was to come, who fulfils the hope of Israel and who will establish the reign of God on earth.
   - *Lord.* This is the title that means that Jesus is King over all, a title given to him after the resurrection.

- Some scholars see, in the reference to the 'heavenly host', the Old Testament idea of the angelic attendants around the throne of God.

   'Where were you when I laid the earth's foundations ... when all the stars of the morning were singing with joy and the sons of God in chorus, were chanting praise'

   (Job 38:4,7).

- This singing with joy rightly gives 'Glory to God' and bestows peace on men who enjoy God's favour. The whole account shows wonder at the birth of this child.

The circumcision and presentation of Jesus (2:21–40)

The brief verse about the circumcision of Jesus is told in a manner similar to that Luke uses when recording the circumcision of John.

The hope of the Jews, that God would send them a Messiah was about to happen. The baby was given the name of Jesus, which means 'God is salvation'.

The Holy Family then went to the Temple to present Jesus to God as required by Jewish law (Exodus 13:1–16). The Law said that every first-born male child should be consecrated or given to God. In this act Luke is saying that God, who sent Jesus to do his work on earth, now consecrates him for that work. That work is one of offering salvation to all people. As part of the ceremony of purification, the mother would be purified, because she would be considered unclean. The ceremonial of the Law required it. She was required to make a sacrifice. Luke records that in Mary's case the offering was that laid down for the poor,

> a pair of turtle doves or two young pigeons (2:24).

THE JEWISH LAW

There were three ceremonies that followed the birth of a male child:

1 *Circumcision*
   This happened on the eighth day after birth. The child received his name.
2 *Presentation*
   This was where the child was consecrated to God and must take place within the first month of the child's life.
3 *Purification*
   The mother was required to offer a sacrifice. This took place on the fortieth day after birth.

It would appear that Luke has confused the latter two into one ceremony.

There were always holy men in the Temple who would take the children into their arms and bless them. One such was Simeon, a devout Jew who had longed all his life to see the

> restoration of Israel (2:25)

What Simeon considered the task of the Christ to be is summed up in the canticle called the *Nunc Dimittis*. In this admirable summary of all Messianic hope, Luke draws once again from the Old Testament, summarising the thoughts of Isaiah (Isaiah 46:13; 49:6; 52:10).

The message of the Nunc Dimittis can be summarised:

- Simeon has seen with his own eyes the Christ.
- The Christ will offer Salvation to all nations.
- The offer will be to the Gentiles as well as the Jews. This is called *Universalism*. It is a favourite theme of Luke in his Gospel.

After blessing Joseph and Mary, Simeon made a strange prophecy.

> This child is destined to be a sign which men reject; and you too shall be pierced to the heart. Many in Israel will stand or fall because of him, and thus the secret thoughts of many will be laid bare *(2:35)*.

This is a difficult saying, because it is one in which Luke attempts to summarise the whole life and work of Jesus.

1 His life will force all men to decide where they stand.
2 Each person will have to face the fact of their own sinfulness and this will strip naked one's secret thoughts.
3 Those who recognise their need of God will be brought to new life. The word used for 'rise' is the one Luke uses only for resurrection. It is Luke's intention to show that the rising of a person to new life in Christ will be completed in the resurrection of the Lord Jesus after his life has been 'a sign which men reject'.

The story comes to an end with Anna, a prophetess, who, like Simeon, looked forward to the liberation of Jerusalem and the coming of the Messiah.

The family returned home to Nazareth. Luke concludes his story with the usual refrain. The child grew strong in wisdom and

God's favour was upon him *(2:40)*.

The boy Jesus in the Temple (2:41–52)

The first twelve years of Jesus' life are passed over in silence. Luke then records a story about Jesus visiting the capital city for the feast of Passover at the age of twelve. The Jewish law required all faithful Jews to make the pilgrimage to Jerusalem three times a year for three different feasts.

1   The feast of Passover which called to mind the Exodus; that moment in Jewish history when the Jews escaped from captivity in Egypt.
2   The feast of Pentecost which remembered the agreement God made with his people in the wanderings in the Sinai desert after their escape from Egypt.
3   The feast of Tabernacles which commemorated how the children of Israel had wandered in the desert and lived in tents (tabernacles), protected and guided by God.

By the time of Jesus, those Jews who lived a distance from Jerusalem were only required to make the pilgrimage at Passover.

On this occasion Mary and Joseph were on their way home before they realised that Jesus was missing. They returned to Jerusalem to search for him.

Luke shows how the close relationship between God and Jesus was already forming in the mind of the young boy. When at last his parents found him sitting amongst the teachers in the Temple and asked him what he was doing, Jesus replied:

> Did you not know that I was bound to be in my Father's house? (2:49).

The story ends with a further comment on the growth of Jesus. In all respects, he continued to grow in wisdom, being prepared for the great work that lay ahead of him.

The importance of the birth of Jesus for Christians today

- *The importance of the birth of Jesus for Christians today cannot be overestimated. They believe that in and through Jesus, God became man. He was born like us. This is what the word 'Incarnation' means. This is a mystery which some people, in every age, have found difficult to accept.*

- *The best way of expressing what Christianity believes about the Incarnation is to look at three views which the early Church refused to accept.*

1 Jesus was not God

Some people claim that Jesus was not really God. There is only one true God. Jesus, while being a great and good man, could not possibly be God. This view was first suggested by a priest called Arius, early in the fourth century. It has been suggested many times since.

- *The Christian Church has always refuted this idea. To Christians, Jesus is 'God from God, light from light . . . one in substance with the Father' (Nicene Creed). In other words, in Jesus, God really appeared on earth as a person.*

2 Jesus the man and Jesus the Son of God are two different people

The second view, unacceptable to Christians, is that the Jesus who lived and walked on earth, two thousand years ago, is not the same person who is called 'Son of God', and who is with God the Father. This view, named after Bishop Nestorius, who lived in the fifth century, is still hinted at by many today. A lot of people seem to refer to Jesus as a good man who lived a long time ago; a man who taught about God and who became Son of God by his resurrection.

- *The Christian Church has always refuted this idea. Jesus the Christ was and is, always, only one person. God is in the man Jesus at all times.*

3   Jesus was God pretending to be a man

The third idea unacceptable to Christians is that Jesus was not really a man but God pretending to be a man. Jesus, therefore, only acted as if he were a man. God lived on earth only in the outward appearance of a man.

- *The Christian Church has always refuted this idea. Christians believe that Jesus had not only a human body but also a human mind and spirit. He was fully human. The real God appeared in a real man.*

Saviour, Christ and Lord

Christians believe that God entered the world in Jesus at Bethlehem. He was born like us, to Mary, in the outhouse of the inn. All Christians would accept the views of Luke and claim that, in Jesus, God has given to the world:

a SAVIOUR,
who is CHRIST and
who is LORD.

Study Skills

Knowledge

1 To whom is the Gospel of Luke dedicated?
2 Who were the parents of John the Baptist?
3 What was the occupation of John the Baptist's father?
4 What words of greeting did the Angel give to Mary when he visited her in Nazareth?
5 What was the message of the Angel to Mary?
6 Name three canticles or sacred songs in the birth stories of Luke.
7 Who was the Roman Emperor at the time of Jesus' birth?
8 Why did Mary and Joseph have to travel from Nazareth to Bethlehem?
9 What message did the Angel give to the shepherds the night Jesus was born?
10 What had Simeon been promised he would see before he died?
11 Which Jewish feast did Jesus celebrate with his parents in Jerusalem when he was twelve years old?
12 What was Jesus doing when his parents found him in the Temple at the end of their search for him?

Understanding

13 What do you understand to be the meaning of the story of the annunciation of the conception of Jesus to Mary?
14 'Today in the city of David, a *deliverer* has been born to you – the *Messiah*, the *Lord*'. What is the meaning of this message? Comment especially on the three words underlined.

Evaluation

15 How important is the birth of Jesus to an understanding of Christianity today?
16 'Today many people have taken the Christ out of Christmas'. Do you agree with this statement? Give reasons for your answer.

Practical Work

• Write a short nativity play for radio based only on Luke's Gospel.
• Design two posters/pictures/charts that show the similarities and differences, in both the announcements of the births and the births themselves, of John the Baptist and Jesus.

3 The Acceptance and Rejection of Jesus

The purpose of this chapter is to examine the differences between the new way of Jesus and the Judaism of the Jewish leaders.

This can be done in contrasting the attitudes of those who accepted Jesus and those who rejected him. The chapter examines the following:
- The attitude of Jesus to the outcast and sinner and their response
  1 the woman who was a sinner (7:36–50)
  2 Zacchaeus (19:1–10)
  3 the Parable of the Great Banquet (14:15–24)
  4 the Parables of the Lost (15:1–32)
  5 the Parable of the Rich Man and Lazarus (16:19–31)
- The attitude of Jesus to the religious leaders and their response
  1 the question of blasphemy (5:17–26)
  2 eating with sinners (5:29–32)
  3 the question of fasting (5:33–35)
  4 working on the sabbath (6:1–5)
  5 healing on the sabbath (6:6–11)
  6 the attack on the Pharisees and Lawyers (11:37–12:3, 20:45–47)
  7 the question of authority (20:1–8)
  8 the question of paying taxes (20:19–26)
  9 the question about resurrection (20:27–38)

The Attitude of Jesus to the Outcast and Sinner and Their Response

Jesus' attitude to the outcast and sinner can be summed up in the comments found in the three parables of the lost. The Pharisees and Doctors of the Law criticised Jesus for welcoming and eating with sinners (15:2). His reply can be found in the three parables of the lost sheep; the lost coin; and the lost son (15:1–32).

> there will be greater joy in heaven over one sinner
> who repents than over ninety-nine righteous people
> who do not need to repent (15:7).

there is joy among the angels of God over one
sinner who repents (*15:10*).

for this son of mine was dead and has come back to
life, he was lost and is found (*15:24*).

In other words, Jesus' message is one of reconciliation; of
telling all people that God welcomes them. Throughout the
Gospel, Jesus welcomes such people into his kingdom. (See
Chapter 4; especially the parable of the great banquet
14:15–24; the parables of the lost 15:1–32; the parable of the
rich man and Lazarus 16:19–31).

The Woman who was a Sinner (7:36–50)

The story
Jesus was invited to dinner at the house of Simon the
Pharisee (see also 11:37; 14:1).

Simon behaved in a rather superior way and did not offer
Jesus the usual courtesies given to a guest. He had not
provided water to wash the feet and had not given him the
traditional greeting of a kiss (7:45). While they were eating, a
woman who had a bad name crept into the room and knelt
at the feet of Jesus. She was crying and began to anoint
Jesus' feet with myrrh which she had brought with her.
Simon criticised Jesus for allowing such an immoral woman
to touch him. The criticism was not made out loud but Jesus
sensed what Simon was thinking.

In reply Jesus told the parable of the two debtors, a simple
story about two men, one of whom owed a lot of money, the
other owed a little. They were both excused their debts by
the creditor.

Which will love him more? (*7:42*).

Meaning
The meaning of the story can be summarised:

(a) the greater the amount of forgiveness, the more grateful is
the person forgiven (7:47).
(b) Simon had little reason to be grateful or even appreciative
of Jesus because he does not have a sense of wrong. He
considered himself to be superior;

where little has been forgiven, little love is shown
(*7:47*).

The foundation stone of love is forgiveness because this can bring people together.

(c) Jesus commented on the woman's actions.

> I tell you, her great love proves that her many sins have been forgiven (7:47).

There is no mention of the occasion when this forgiveness had taken place. Perhaps the woman had already met Jesus previously and had changed her immoral life, and in so doing, had realised that her sins had been forgiven and was now showing gratitude for this.

(d) Jesus confirmed this forgiveness.

> Your sins are forgiven (7:48).

Immediately this was questioned by the other guests as, according to the Jews, only God had the authority to forgive sins. Jesus ignored their murmurings. He was more concerned with the woman.

> Your faith has saved you: Go in peace (7:50).

Interpretation for today

Christians today believe that Jesus has the authority to forgive sins. They would also claim that such forgiveness is important in their lives, for without the forgiveness of God and each other, it is seen as impossible to be reconciled with God.

Some Christians, notably those belonging to the Roman Catholic Tradition, receive the Sacrament of Reconciliation, popularly called 'Confession'. Within this sacrament, a person may, through the intermediary of the priest, confess sins to God, and receive God's absolution. Other churches do not see the need for such a sacramental structure and urge their people to ask God directly for the forgiveness of sins.

Zacchaeus 19:1–10

The story

Zacchaeus was a tax-collector and was therefore very unpopular with the Jews, not only because he worked for the Romans but also because he was very rich through cheating people, as he himself admitted (19:8).

This little man wanted to see Jesus and climbed a sycamore tree to get a better view. Jesus had probably been told about Zacchaeus and so was able to call him by name. He told him that he wanted to stay with him. This action received the usual disapproval, although for once, not from the Jewish leaders but from the crowd in general. This shows the extent to which Zacchaeus was disliked.

Zacchaeus made a public confession of his past and declared he was ready to make amends. He volunteered to do two things:

– to give half his property to charity; and
– to repay those he had cheated fourfold.

After this, no one could call Zacchaeus a sinner again. He was restored to his rightful place in the Jewish community, for he was a 'son of Abraham' (19:9).

   Salvation has come to this house today (19:9).

Meaning
The important truth about this story is not that Zacchaeus had a change of heart as though he had suddenly decided that the way back to God was through good works of charity. Zacchaeus became reconciled to God because Jesus, instead of ignoring him or treating him like an outcast, had deliberately gone out of his way to meet and befriend him.

Interpretation for today

Christians believe that when a person meets Jesus they can turn their back on the past and return to a life with God. They believe this meeting with Jesus can happen in many ways; through the love of friend or family; through other human relationships; through the Church; through the scriptures, to name but some of the ways.

They also believe that, like Zacchaeus, many people who have come back to God, desire to make amends for their past. This need not follow the pattern laid down by Zacchaeus but can be something as simple as turning the back on the past and seeking reconciliation with God and other people.

The Parable of the Great Banquet 14:15–24
(see Chapter 4)
The Parables of the Lost 15:1–32
(see Chapter 4)
The Parable of the Rich Man and Lazarus 16:19–31
(see Chapter 4)

The Attitude of Jesus to the Religious Leaders and Their Response

There is no suggestion in Luke's Gospel that Jesus thought of the Jewish leaders as being evil men. The Pharisees, Sadducees, Scribes and Priests were honourable men who believed passionately in their interpretation of religion. It is important to remember that Luke's Gospel shows the belief of the first century Christians. They believed that Jesus had been sent by God to call all people, especially the Jews, back to himself. But the Jewish leaders rejected Jesus. The Gospel comments clearly on this growing source of conflict that was to lead to Jesus' death.

The source of the conflict is to be found in Jesus' attitude to the Jewish authorities. This can be summed up in one word, 'hypocrisy'. The word, in Greek, means 'actor'. In Jesus' day, as in our own, it came to mean someone who does not 'practise what they preach'; someone who plays out a role that is not really themselves. When Jesus used the word of the religious leaders he meant that they were not being true to the faith and practice of the religion they professed. They had lost their way.

In addition, they had misled the ordinary people and made religion a burden. They had made it virtually impossible for the sinner to return to God. It is this latter point that made Jesus most angry.

The Question of Blasphemy 5:17–26

This story is concerned with the healing of the paralysed man (see Chapter 5).

Eating with Sinners 5:29–32

The Problem
The Pharisees and lawyers would not eat with the ordinary people. They would not even mix with such sinners as tax collectors because they considered them to be immoral. Jesus had called Levi to be a disciple and in gratitude Levi invited Jesus to a meal at his house. Naturally other guests present were Levi's friends who were also tax collectors. The Pharisees and lawyers considered that Jesus was wrong to eat in such company because he was in the company of people who would not be tolerated by strict Jews.

The Reply of Jesus
The answer of Jesus both condemned the religious leaders and also explained the purpose of his mission. If the Pharisees and lawyers thought themselves to be so perfect that they were not aware of their own sin, then little could be done for them. If they were self-sufficient, then they were not open to God. They were outwardly religious but their hearts were far from God. Jesus pointed out that he had not come for such 'virtuous' people but to give hope to those who knew they were in need.

It is not the healthy that need a doctor but the sick; I have not come to invite virtuous people, but to call sinners to repentance *(5:31–2).*

Fasting 5:33–35

The Problem
Fasting was demanded of all Jews on one day in the year. This was called the 'Day of Atonement'. This fast was when the Jews asked God for his forgiveness. The only other time the Jews were required to fast was at times of national disaster such as famine or war. At all other times fasting was a matter of personal conscience. The practice of fasting had grown up amongst the Pharisees as a sign of their superiority. They thought it was pleasing to God. So, by the time of Jesus they fasted on Mondays and Thursdays.

Jesus' disciples are criticised for not fasting as the Pharisees did. The inference is that they were rather keen on eating and drinking.

The Reply of Jesus
The reply of Jesus makes it quite clear that the time for fasting had not yet arrived. He used the illustration of a wedding and asked the question,

Can you make the bridegroom's friends fast while the bridegroom is with them? *(5:34).*

In other words, nobody fasts at a wedding. Jesus compared himself to the bridegroom. While he was still with them, it was to be a time of celebration and joy. The time would come soon enough when the bridegroom would be taken away. Then they could fast. This is a reference to the crucifixion.

Working on the Sabbath 6:1–5

The Problem
According to the book of Genesis, God created the world in six days and rested on the Sabbath. The Jews, therefore, regarded the Sabbath as a day of rest.

By the time of Jesus this noble idea had been developed into 513 different points of law with detailed conditions to cover every possible situation. The law stated, for example, that no work could be done on the Sabbath. Work was carefully defined under thirty-nine headings. Some of the kinds of work not allowed on the Sabbath were such things as sowing; reaping; threshing; preparing food and carrying a burden. Jesus and his disciples were accused by some Pharisees of reaping, threshing and eating food prepared on the Sabbath. All they had done was to pick ears of corn as they walked along, rub them in their hands and eat the grain.

The Reply of Jesus
Jesus replied, using a method of argument well known to the Jews. He referred to an Old Testament story in which King David had broken the law when it was necessary to feed his retreating and hungry troops. Jesus claimed that the

Son of Man is sovereign even over the Sabbath (6:5).

In other words, as God's representative on earth, Jesus has the authority to break the Sabbath law.

Healing on the Sabbath 6:6–11

This story is concerned with the healing of the man with the withered hand (see Chapter 5).

SUMMARY

These five stories are grouped together by Luke to show that Jesus received opposition from the religious authorities at the beginning of his ministry. The stories highlight the five different claims of Jesus that set him against the religious leaders and pointed the way to understand his teaching:

... the Son of Man has the right on earth to forgive sins (5:24)

I have not come to invite virtuous people but sinners ... (5:32)

Can you make the bridegroom's friends fast while the bridegroom is still with them? (5:34)

The Son of Man is sovereign even over the Sabbath (6:5)

Is it permitted to do good or to do evil on the Sabbath; to save life or to destroy it? (6:9)

Interpretation for today

Sometimes some Christians are misunderstood. Some people think they are like the Pharisees who live by a strict set of rules and regulations. They see the Church as something negative; people whose main cry is 'you must not do this and you must not do that'. They also accuse Christians of thinking that they are morally superior and taking great delight in this so-called virtue.

Many Christians would admit that the Church, at times, gives this impression, but they would stress that this is a false impression.

Rather, Christians believe that every individual is of value to God and to each other. Christianity is a positive message in which proper behaviour is a vital part of the relationship with God and with each other. This relationship is based on love. It is not a relationship in which rules are kept for their own sake, out of either fear of punishment or hope of reward.

The Attack on the Pharisees and Lawyers 11:37–12:3; 20:45–47

The Problem
Jesus had been invited to dine at the house of a Pharisee (see 7:36; 14:1). The Pharisee noticed that Jesus had not washed before the meal. This was not a question of hygiene but a matter of religious practice. The Pharisees took great care to wash their hands in a special ceremonial way, allowing an eggshell of water to run from the fingers to the elbow. They performed this ceremony as a sign that they were holy and

consecrated to God. So, if they had come into contact, however small, with a Gentile or even ordinary Jews they would perform this action as a means of purification.

It would seem that, on this occasion, their criticism of Jesus was too much, for he launched a fierce attack on them. The passage divides into two parts. In the first part Jesus attacked the Pharisees on three counts; in the second, he turned his criticism to the lawyers on a further three matters.

The Reply of Jesus Against the Pharisees
(a) **Ritual washing** (11:37–41) The ceremonial washing carried out by the Pharisees applied not just to the person but also to all drinking and cooking vessels and utensils.

Jesus attacked the Pharisees for their outward observance of the Law without paying due attention to matters of inner meaning, the matters of the heart.

> you clean the outside of cup and plate but inside
> there is nothing but greed and wickedness (*11:39*)

In other words, the Pharisees observed all the external regulations of their religion while remaining extremely selfish and wicked. They should concentrate on putting the heart right and then the religious practices will have an end beyond the mere ceremonial.

(b) **Tithes** (11:42) A tithe was one-tenth of a person's income from all things, which was to be given to God each year. This was a good law and Jesus did not condemn the Pharisees for keeping it (11:42). Once again, however, the Pharisees took the law literally and applied it to every little thing including weighing out a tenth of their garden herbs. Jesus criticised them for having such a strict attitude to what was, after all, a relatively unimportant detail, while at the same time not giving the same attention to the much more important matters of

> justice and the love of God (*11:41*).

This comment by Jesus is a reference to the words of Micah in the Old Testament:

> 'God has told you what is good;
> and what it is that the Lord asks of you?
> Only to act justly, to love loyalty,
> to walk wisely before your God' (Micah 6:8).

(c) **Seats of honour** (11:43–44) The Pharisees loved to receive the praise of ordinary people. They enjoyed the special seats reserved for them in the synagogue which were at the front in full view of the rest of the congregation. They enjoyed the greetings of ordinary people in the street. Jesus turned on them:

> Alas, you are like unmarked graves over which men may walk without knowing it (*11:44*).

To touch a grave, even without realising it, made a Jew unclean. Jesus is saying that the Pharisees are leading innocent people astray. (The same criticism is made against the lawyers in 20:45–47).

Rather foolishly, a lawyer tried to defend the Pharisees (11:45), but only succeeded in giving Jesus an opportunity to turn his attention to the lawyers.

The reply of Jesus against the lawyers
(a) **Burdens** (11:46) The lawyers were the ones who had worked out the oral law (see Chapter 1), with all its minute rules and regulations, which made it virtually impossible for the ordinary people to keep to it. The lawyers had done nothing to help people in their frustration and difficulty.
(b) **Tombs of the prophets** (11:47–51) This is a difficult passage to interpret. The prophets were honoured by the lawyers who had built elaborate tombs and memorials to them, even though the prophets had been killed by the lawyers' ancestors. The inference is that more attention should have been given to the message of the prophets when they were alive, and not to obscure their significance and message by dwelling on unimportant details.

The origin of the quotation in 11:49 is unknown. Neither Abel or Zechariah were prophets, although they were the first and last deaths in the Jewish scriptures. Jesus is saying that now is the day of reckoning. The Jewish leaders of the day will have to answer for the wrongs of the past. The time for decision has come in the person of Jesus himself.
(c) **Key of knowledge** (11:52) This criticism carries the same meaning as the earlier one concerning burdens (11:46). This time the illustration used is that of the key of knowledge. The lawyers had obscured the simple knowledge of God with excess trimmings and so prevented people from seeing the simple truth that God wishes all to return to him.

At this point Jesus left the Pharisee's house and the Pharisees and lawyers, in their anger, began to ask him questions designed to trap him (11:53–54). A crowd gathered and Jesus took one last opportunity to speak to his disciples about the Pharisees.

> Beware of the leaven of the Pharisees: I mean their hypocrisy (*12:1*).

The word 'leaven' in this context means 'evil'. There will come a time when they will be seen for what they are; hypocrites!

Interpretation for today

Hypocrisy is still a danger which Christians have to face. The dangers can be listed quite clearly:

- *Christians must not consider themselves to be morally or spiritually superior to others.*
- *They must never forget that the relationship with God is a matter of the heart and not an outward show of ceremonial piety.*
- *The Christian must have a deep love of God and justice for all people.*
- *Christians must not consider themselves to be worthy of respect. They must not lead people astray by pretending to be better than anyone else.*
- *Christians must make every effort to welcome people who are seeking God. They must never put barriers in the way.*
- *Above all, Christians must not pretend to be better than they are, for that is what makes for hypocrisy.*

The Question about Authority 20:1–8

Just as at the beginning of the Gospel in Galilee, Luke gathered five stories together to show the difference in attitude between Jesus and the religious authorities (5:17–6:11), so in the period of the Jerusalem ministry he includes three stories where the authorities ask Jesus questions designed to trap him. This shows the mounting opposition to Jesus just prior to his arrest.

The Problem
The first of the three questions is asked by the priests, lawyers and elders. Jesus is in the Temple teaching when

they challenge him. It is not surprising that such a challenge was made for, after all, Jesus had challenged their own authority in driving out the traders from the Temple (19:45–46).

The question they asked was:

> Tell us by what authority you are acting like this;
> who gave you this authority? (20:2).

Whatever reply Jesus gave would have placed him in danger. If he had said his authority was from God he would have laid himself open to the charge of blasphemy. If he had claimed he was acting in his own name, he would have been made to look ridiculous.

The Reply of Jesus
Jesus refused to answer either way. Instead he asked them a question in return:

> was the baptism of John from God or from men?
> (20:4).

The phrase, the baptism of John, summed up all John the Baptist's work. He had called people to repentance and had baptised those who had responded.

The questioners were not placed in the same difficulty as Jesus had been in. If they said John was an ordinary man acting on his own authority, they would have made the people angry, for they regarded John as a prophet and a prophet received his authority from God. If they said that John's authority came from God then they would have been criticised for not listening to him. They refused to answer which allowed Jesus to refuse to answer their original question.

Interpretation for today

It would be a mistake to think that Jesus was just being evasive in the way he treated the question of authority. Christians see, in his answer, that Jesus was stating where his authority came from. He had been baptised by John and his authority stemmed from that moment for the voice of God had said to him:

> Thou art my Son, my Beloved; on thee my favour
> rests (3:22).

The question about paying taxes 20:19–26

The problem
The priests and lawyers were anxious to arrest Jesus but were afraid of the people's reaction. So they sent secret agents to listen to him hoping to find some evidence by which he might be reported to the Governor (20:19–20). In the end they put their own question to him to try and trap him:

> Are we or are we not permitted to pay taxes to the Roman Emperor? (*20:22*).

The tax in question was a poll-tax imposed by the Romans in 6 AD. It was extremely unpopular because it symbolised Roman rule. Once again, Jesus was faced with the problem of answering. If he said 'Yes', he would have become unpopular with the people, who hated the tax. If he said 'No', he would be committing treason against Rome and could be arrested and brought before the Roman authorities.

The Reply of Jesus
Jesus called for a coin and asked whose head and inscription was printed on it. When they said 'Caesar's', his reply was:

> Pay Caesar what is due to Caesar, and pay God what is due to God (*20:25*).

What Jesus meant by this reply was that the Jews, by using Roman coins, recognised the Romans as the state authority. Therefore, they must recognise civil authority. In addition to this authority, however, there was the further allegiance owing to God.

Interpretation for today
There have, throughout history, been many periods of tension between Church and State. Most Christians today would accept that the Church and the State must exist side by side. The state has the right to make demands on such things as taxes, but it has no right to make demands that would conflict with a Christian's allegiance to God. If there is a conflict between duty to the state and duty to God, then Christians would claim that God and his demands must come first.

The Question about Resurrection 20:27–38

The Problem
The third question was asked by the Sadducees. They asked

a question about resurrection even though they themselves did not believe in it. The question was based on an ancient Jewish law called the Levirate law (Deuteronomy 25:5–6). The purpose of this law, which was not widely practised at the time of Jesus, was to preserve both a family line and the inheritance of family wealth.

The question was a rather extreme example. There were seven brothers. The first married and died childless. The second, third, fourth and so on, one by one, married the widow and each died childless. Finally, the widow herself died. Whose wife will she be at the resurrection?

The Reply of Jesus
Jesus' reply covered two distinct topics.
1 **At the resurrection people do not marry**.
Jesus is saying that there is no need for marriage in heaven. It is an earthly institution that ends at death.
2. **There is a resurrection**.
Jesus claimed this truth was implied in the Old Testament. When God appeared to Moses at the time of the burning bush, he told Moses, 'I am the God of Abraham, the God of Isaac and the God of Jacob'. These three Jewish leaders were long since dead but God spoke of them as still being alive.

Interpretation for today

Christians today would accept both these points of teaching without question. They accept that marriage is an earthly institution which ends at death. This is made very clear in the rite of marriage where a couple enter into marriage 'till death do us part'.

In the same way, Christians accept the fact of resurrection as being fundamental to Christian belief. They do not believe that death is the end but that there is a life beyond death.

Study Skills

Knowledge

1 Whose house was Jesus in when he was anointed by the sinful woman?
2 Why did the woman anoint Jesus?
3 What was the occupation of Zacchaeus?
4 Why did Jesus want to stay with Zacchaeus?

5 Why was Jesus accused of being blasphemous when he healed the paralysed man?

6 What did Jesus say in answer to the criticism that he was mixing with sinners in Levi's house?

7 How did the disciples break the Sabbath law when they were walking through the cornfields?

8 How did Jesus answer the question 'Tell us by what authority you are acting like this'?

9 What did Jesus say when he was asked if it was permitted to pay taxes to Caesar?

10 What was the Levirate law?

Understanding

11 What do you understand to be the teaching of Jesus in the story of the anointing of Jesus by the woman who was a sinner?

12 What do you understand to be new about Jesus' teaching on the subject of the Sabbath law?

Evaluation

13 Why do you think that people such as the sinful woman and Zacchaeus responded to Jesus?

14 Choose two occasions when Jesus disagreed with the Pharisees. Give both sides of the argument and state which side you agree with and the reasons why.

Examination Practice

Describe what happened when Jesus went for a meal at the house of Simon the Pharisee.   (6)

Name one other occasion when Jesus forgave sins in Luke's Gospel.   (2)

Why do you think Jesus opposed the Pharisees?   (6)

Does the difference in Jesus' and the Pharisees' attitudes to religion have any relevance for Christians today?   (6)

Practical work

Find out all you can about the Pharisees and Scribes. Present this information on large sheets of paper for display. Underline all the points in which Jesus came into conflict with the Pharisees and Scribes. Produce a section on the display in which the teaching of Jesus is shown.

4 The Parables of the Kingdom of God

The purpose of this chapter is to look at the parables of the kingdom of God in Luke's Gospel. The following topics will be examined:

– What is a parable?
– What is an allegory?
– Why did Jesus use parables?
– The kingdom of God.
– *The meaning of the kingdom of God for today.*
– The parables and their meaning for today.

– The kingdom of God has arrived
  1 The Parables of the Patches and Wineskins (5:36–39).
  2 The Parable of the Sower (8:4–8; 11–15).
  3 The Parable of the Lamp (8:16–17).
  4 The Parables of the Mustard Seed and Yeast (13:18–21).

– Repentance and forgiveness is the way into the kingdom
  5 The Parable of the Two Debtors (7:41–43).
  6 The Parable of the Wedding Guests (14:7–11).
  7 The Parable of the Great Banquet (14:12–24).
  8 The Parables of the Lost Sheep; the Lost Coin; the Lost Son (15:1–32).
  9 The Parable of the Pharisee and the Tax-collector (18:9–14).

– The claims of the kingdom
  10 The Parable of the Good Samaritan (10:25–37).
  11 The Parables of the Friend at Midnight (11:5–13) and The Unjust Judge (18:1–8).
  12 The Parable of the Crafty Steward (16:1–8).

– The crisis of the kingdom
  13 The Parables of the Rich Fool (12:13–21); The Watchful Servants (12:35–38); The Burglar (12:39) and The Faithful and Unfaithful Servants (12:42–46).
  14 The Barren Fig Tree (13:6–9).
  15 The Rich Man and Lazarus (16:19–31).

16   The Parable of the Pounds (19:11–27).
17   The Parable of the Wicked Husbandmen (20:9–19).

What is a Parable?

A parable is a simple story with a single, simple meaning. It has one central point of teaching and the details of the story make that point both clear and vivid. The meaning is not explained but is left for the listeners to work out for themselves.

A true parable relates to real life. They have a Palestinian background. The events and characters are drawn from everyday life.

Parables are the method of teaching Jesus used.

What is an Allegory?

In contrast, an allegory is a story where the message is hidden in a type of code; where the characters and/or events really represent other characters and events; a story where every detail has a meaning. An allegory may depart from everyday life into a make-believe world. The story has to be decoded in order to understand its meaning.

Some scholars believe that the allegories or allegorical interpretation of the parables were the creation of either the early Christians, or of the Evangelists themselves, reflecting the belief of the churches for whom they were writing.

Why did Jesus use Parables?

1   Jesus used parables because they are simple stories, easy both to listen to and understand.
2   The Jews were used to listening to parables as this method of teaching was well established in their culture.
3   At a time when most learning was by word of mouth, the short story was easily remembered.
4   The hearers have to interpret the parables for themselves. This gave them a deeper meaning and importance. The interpretation became part of a person's experience.
5   There is, however, an answer by Luke, to the question 'why did Jesus teach by using parables?' that is hard to understand.

He claims that the reason Jesus taught in parables was to confuse people.

> It has been granted to you to know the secrets of
> the kingdom of God; but the others have only
> parables, in order that they may look but see
> nothing, hear but understand nothing (*8:10*).

These verses seem to be saying that the disciples understand
because they have been given the secrets of the kingdom but
everybody else is taught in parables so that it will confuse
them and prevent them from coming into the kingdom. This
is a problem.

The reason Jesus used parables cannot have been to hide
the truth from people because this is not the intention of
teaching and it seems out of character with what we learn
about Jesus elsewhere in the Gospel. There must be another
answer to this problem. Various suggestions have been made.

1   The verses, loosely based on Isaiah 6:9–10, are meant to
    explain the fact that the disciples responded to Jesus but
    there were many who refused to repent and stand outside
    because they do not recognise who Jesus is.
2   The early Christians believed that it was God's plan for
    the Jews to reject Jesus so that his death and resurrection
    could unite all people with God.
3   The verses were added to explain why the early Church's
    teaching was rejected by the Jews.

It would seem that the most likely explanation is that Luke
believed the purpose of the parables was to hide the truth
from those whose hearts were already set against
Christianity. In so doing, he has given a false picture of
Jesus' own intention in the use of parables.

The Kingdom of God

The theme of all the parables is the central theme of the
Gospel; the meaning of the kingdom of God.

The Jews used the phrase, kingdom of God, to refer to the
power and authority of God. They never used it to mean an
earthly kingdom in the sense of an area of land which was
ruled by God.

It was more a question of belonging to God's kingdom by
responding to him in faith and accepting his 'rule' over one's
life.

The Jews looked at the kingdom of God in two different
ways:

1   The kingdom of God was **PRESENT** in the sense that God guided his people at all times.
2   The kingdom of God will come in the **FUTURE** in the sense that God will be accepted by the whole world and his rule established on the earth.

The Jews believed that God controlled everything; the forces of nature; Israelities as his chosen people and also the destiny of all other nations.

They looked forward to that future time when God's rule would be all over the earth. Some of them believed that it would be brought about by an ideal representative of God, an anointed one, a Messiah (see Chapter 9). Jesus says such a moment has arrived.

The first words of Jesus in Luke's Gospel show how Jesus claims to be the anointed one. He quotes the prophet Isaiah:

> The Spirit of the Lord is upon me because he has anointed me (*4:18*).

The anointed one was to bring

> good news to the poor; . . .
> proclaim release for prisoners and recovery of sight for the blind; . . .
> to proclaim the year of the Lord's favour, . .

which is another way of saying,

> proclaim the kingdom of God (4:17–19).

Jesus went on to say that what Isaiah had prophesied has come true. It had come true in Jesus himself.

The meaning of the kingdom of God for today

The idea of the kingdom of God is still relevant to Christians even though the term is not widely used today. They still believe that the kingdom of God is something present in the lives of men and women.

Some say that to belong to the kingdom of God is the same as belonging to the Church.

Others claim that to belong to the kingdom of God is not exactly the same as being a member of the Church. Being a member of the kingdom goes beyond simply belonging to any individual Church. They believe the kingdom of God is to do with the whole person. It is the dedication of the whole of life to God.

The parables of the kingdom, therefore, are still seen as relevant today by all Christians. They may be set in the everyday life of two thousand years ago and, therefore, seem somewhat remote from modern times but the meaning of them is still true.

The Parables and their Meaning for today

The parables of Luke's Gospel can be divided into four main groups, all of which comment in some way on the major theme of the kingdom of God.

– *The kingdom of God has arrived.*
– *The way into the kingdom is through repentance and forgiveness.*
– *The claims of the kingdom.*
– *The crisis of the kingdom.*

The kingdom of God has arrived

The Parables of The New Cloth and New Wine (5:36–39)

This is what is known as a 'double parable' or 'doublet'. That is where there are two parables side by side with identical meanings.

Luke has rewritten a saying he has found in Mark's Gospel but in the re-writing he loses some of the significance.

Compare these two extracts:

Mark	Luke
No one sews a piece of unshrunk cloth on to an old coat; if he does, the patch tears away from it, the new from the old, and leaves a bigger hole (Mark 2:21)	No one tears a piece from a new cloak to patch an old one; if he does, he will have made a hole in the new cloak, and the patch from the new will not match the old (5:36)

Mark's original version begins, 'No one sews a piece of unshrunk cloth on to an old coat . . .' This is good advice and every Jewish woman would know this. No one, however, would even think of doing what Luke suggests; tearing a piece off a new garment to sew onto an old one.

Jesus is pointing out how foolish it is to sew a patch of unshrunken material onto an old garment or to put new wine, still fermenting, into old skins that have lost their pliability and have become brittle.

Meaning

1 A garment was a common symbol for the world. The Jewish religion was worn out and could no longer be patched.
2 Wine was a common symbol for salvation. Jesus had not come to reform Judaism but to present something new and revolutionary.

In simple terms, therefore, the old Judaism and the new Christianity will not mix. There is something new and different in the ministry of Jesus that goes beyond the boundaries of Judaism. What is new is summed up by the phrase,

> The kingdom of God is here!.

If this is the meaning of the two parables then Luke spoils the effect of adding an original verse at the end.

> And no one after drinking old wine wants new; for he says, 'The old wine is good' (5:39).

This verse raises difficulties. It would seem that Luke is saying that the old is better. Surely Luke cannot be claiming that Judaism is better than Christianity? There are two possible interpretations of this difficult verse:

1 Luke might be saying that those who are rigid in their views of the past will not be able to accept the new way.
2 Luke, by inserting this verse, is suggesting a cautious rejection of the old way. The new must contain the good elements of the old, such as the Law.

The meaning of the parable for today

- *Christians see, in the Parable of the Patches and Wineskins, that the kingdom of God is present here and now in the lives of people who have responded to the message of Jesus.*

  Just as the new piece of cloth would not suit the torn old cloak and the new wine would burst the old wineskins, so the kingdom of God must call for a new understanding of the message of Jesus for peoples' lives.

The Parable of the Sower 8:4–8; 11–15

The Parable of the Sower is one of the most well known of all the parables. The seed falls on four different types of soil; the footpath, rocky ground, among thistles and on good soil. At first sight this may be seen as careless farming with so much seed being wasted.

The parable, however, only makes sense when seen against the method of farming followed in Palestine at that time. Certainly some seed was wasted but this is exactly what used to happen. The sowing was done before the ploughing.

Meaning

A few verses later, after the account of the parable, Luke gives an allegorical meaning (8:11–15). But what would the interpretation be if that allegorical answer was not printed for all to see? It would be regarded as a simple parable, which shows, on the one hand, the frustrations of the sower's labouring; with its weeds, greedy birds and rocky ground; and on the other hand, in contrast to this, a picture of a rich harvest.

The meaning of this simple story is that the kingdom of God will be successful in spite of all frustrations and difficulties.

The allegorical interpretation of the parable is given in the Gospel. There are four such different kinds of soil representing four types of hearer of the message of Jesus.

1 *The unresponsive hearer*
   Satan carries off the word giving the person no chance to respond.
2 *The shallow hearer*
   The person who has no roots, lacking depth and persistence.
3 *The worldly hearer*
   The person who is seduced by the pleasures of the world.
4 *The responsive hearer*
   The person who, living a life of faith, obtains depth, according to his faith.

There is something very unsatisfying about this explanation of the parable. Many scholars believe that this interpretation is not original and was not given by Jesus. They believe that the interpretation is from a later period of the Church and that it arises from using the parable for teaching purposes.

Under self-examination, a person is required to ask, 'What kind of soil am I?'. Such an interpretation misses the original and simple truth of the parable.

The meaning of the parable for today

- *The parable of the sower is still relevant today. There have been many times in history when Christianity has faced extreme difficulty. Sometimes it has been persecution or suppression. At other times it has been treated with apathy. Throughout, the kingdom of God has not only survived but flourished. Christians of all nations and of every colour and race have found faith in Christ to be the centre of their lives.*
- *The allegorical interpretation of the parable also continues to have meaning. The comparison of people with different types of soil may seem strange today but the idea of examining one's own faith is a good one. Christians need to reflect from time to time on their faith, knowing that it is easy to be distracted from their calling to be disciples.*

The Parable of the Lamp 8:16–17

A lamp is not hidden under a bed or covered with a basin. The only purpose for a lamp is for it to give out light so that people can see.

Meaning
These verses are a comment on hearing and learning. Hearing is meant to lead to understanding. To hear without understanding is like lighting a lamp and covering it with a basin so that it cannot shine.

The parable is a criticism of the Jewish teachers who have hidden the kingdom of God instead of revealing it to the people.

The meaning of the parable for today

- *All Christians would testify to the modern day relevance of the Parable of the Lamp. They are able to point to the lives of famous Christian men and women whose lives have shone with the light of Christ. What is perhaps even more important is that they would also be able to name thousands of unknown and ordinary people, who, by their kindness, advice and example, have shown what it means to be a Christian.*

The Parable of the Mustard Seed and the Yeast 13:18–21

These two parables are, in many ways, the simplest of all the parables.

The mustard seed is the smallest seed of all but when it is planted, it grows into a tree. The mustard seed produces a shrub about eight to ten feet tall with branches strong enough to support and give birds shelter.

The example of the yeast follows the same pattern. A small pinch of yeast added to the flour produces a dough that will rise well beyond its former size.

Meaning
1   It is exactly the same with the kingdom of God. From small beginnings it will grow into a vast kingdom of God.
2   These were common metaphors for a great kingdom to be established by the Messiah. Jesus gathered a small band of followers, and through God's power, they were to become the people of God in the kingdom of God.

The meaning of the parables for today

- *The parables of the mustard seed and the yeast can be seen as in the process of being fulfilled. From the beginnings of Christianity in the first century, the movement has continued to spread until it now embraces every continent on earth. From these small beginnings it has grown into something large. Christians believe the growth will continue until the daily prayer which Jesus taught his disciples becomes a reality. 'Your kingdom come! Your will be done on earth as it is in heaven'.*

Repentance and Forgiveness is the Way into the Kingdom

The Parable of the Two Debtors 7:41–43 (see Chapter 3)

The Parable of the Wedding Guests 14:7–11

Jesus was at a meal in the house of one of the leading Pharisees and had just cured a man suffering from dropsy (14:1–6). He noticed that some of the guests were trying to take the best seats at the meal. Jesus told this parable about social etiquette. When invited to dinner do not sit in the places of honour as there may well be a more distinguished guest present for whom the place has been reserved. In order to avoid embarrassment, always take the lowest seat. Then you may well be invited to a more important place.

Meaning
The Pharisees loved to have the places of honour on every possible occasion. Jesus considered that this high opinion of oneself conflicted with a person's place before God. In other words a person who thinks they are superior has little awareness of their need of God and finds repentance and forgiveness hard to understand. Those who judge themselves to be of higher rank will be disappointed for they are far from the kingdom of God.

The meaning of the parable for today

This parable is as meaningful to Christians today, as it has always been. They would claim that there is no place in Christianity for those who seek superiority of position. If such behaviour does take place within Christianity, then it has become distorted. Christians still believe that their faith demands that they put other people first in all things.

The Parable of the Great Banquet 14:12–24

While Jesus was at the same dinner (14:1), he told his host that true happiness could be found by inviting those people to a meal who could not return the compliment, such as the poor, crippled, lame and blind (14:12–14). This led one of the guests to say

> Happy the man who shall sit at the feast in the kingdom of God.

Jesus told the parable of the great banquet in reply.

A man gave a big dinner party and sent out many invitations. Some of the guests made excuses. So the host sent out into the town and then into the country to invite others to take their places. None of the original guests would get a taste of the banquet.

Meaning
This parable has been developed into an allegory.
- The symbol of the banquet stands for the kingdom of God. It was a popular image of the Messianic kingdom.

- The guests who had been invited had plenty of time to
  make the necessary arrangements. After accepting they all
  made rather weak excuses. The piece of land could be
  seen anytime. The same applied to the new oxen. Even
  the excuse of just getting married was rude. Surely the
  wedding could have been arranged for another time,
  having first accepted a longstanding invitation.
  Interpretation
  The people making the excuses are obviously the Jewish
  leaders who have rejected the invitation to enter God's
  kingdom.
- The invitation is not given to the poor, the crippled, the
  blind, and the lame of the town.
  Interpretation
  These people stand for the Jewish sinner or outcast.
- There is still room and the servant is sent further afield
  into the countryside to bring others in.
  Interpretation
  These people stand for the Gentiles.

This parable shows clearly Luke's theme of *Universalism*. The
Jewish leaders had rejected the invitation of God. Now the
kingdom will be given to those who acknowledge their need
of God, both Jew and Gentile alike.

The meaning of the parable for today

*Christians believe that the message of the Gospel is for all people.
They would claim that the kingdom of God is open to all,
regardless of race, colour or class. The parable of the great
banquet, with its emphasis on the universalism of the Gospel, is
seen as being totally relevant to a modern understanding of
Christianity.*

The Parables of the Lost Sheep; the Lost Coin; the Lost Son (15:1–32)

Jesus told these three parables because, once again, he had
been criticised by the Pharisees and Doctors of the Law for
mixing with sinners.

The doublet of the Lost Sheep and the Lost Coin are
simple in form. Both rely on something lost being found, a
sheep in the first parable and a silver coin in the second.

The parable of the Lost Son is much more involved, but
still follows the same principle that the son who was lost is

found again. Unlike the lost sheep and the lost coin, the son is lost through his own deliberate choice. The parable has certain allegorical elements about it.

The lost son.....................................the sinner
The father ....God
The elder son....................................the Scribes and Pharisees

The lost son

(a) He squandered his money on the indulgence of all his desires. He became a sinner.
(b) When he had spent all his money he found himself alone and destitute. He sold himself to a local pig farmer. Pigs are 'unclean' to the Jew. This detail in the story shows that the son was driven to the depths of despair. He sat amongst the pigs, so hungry that he was tempted to eat the pigs' swill. He experienced what sin does to a person. He felt completely separated from life.

   Then he came to his senses.

(c) 'Then he came to his senses'. The young man had reached the lowest point of despair. He knew he was a sinner. He knew he deserved nothing and so he decided to go home and throw himself on his father's mercy.
(d) He returned home rehearsing what he would say to his father.

Meaning
This is a wonderful illustration of how a person strays from God and from his fellow human beings. His actions result in him being utterly and completely lost. This is what sin does to a person.

The father

(a) The son did not believe that there was any possibility of his father forgiving him. He was relying on the hope that he might, at least, become a servant back in his father's house. He did not expect forgiveness.

   But while he was still a long way off . . .

(b) The father had never stopped loving his son. Anxiously, he spent the days watching and waiting, constantly looking down the road, longing for his return. At last he saw him and ran to meet him and joyfully welcomed him.

The son did not even get a chance to finish his prepared speech. The father cut him off in mid-sentence in his eagerness to forgive.

> Quick! fetch a robe, my best one, and put it on him; put a ring on his finger and shoes on his feet ...

The symbols of sonship were restored without reservation.

> For this son of mine was dead and has come back to life; he was lost and is found.

Meaning
Most people see in the actions of the father a picture of God's forgiveness. Jesus is saying that God forgives the sinner absolutely. There are no conditions attached. God longs for all people to come to him like the son returned to the father in the parable.

The elder son

(a) The elder son was working for the father as usual. When he heard that his brother had returned and had been welcomed back he was angry. After all, his brother had wasted all his money 'with his women'. He deserved nothing.
(b) The father pleaded with the elder brother and tried to point out to him that it was only right to celebrate for it was as if the younger son had come back to life from the dead.

Meaning
Some people feel a certain sympathy with the elder son. He had slaved away. He had been obedient and had never received the fuss that was being made over the return of his brother. He shows the typical standard of human forgiveness and in so doing mirrors exactly the attitude of the Pharisees and Scribes to the poor and outcast of Jesus' day. The forgiveness they offered fell far short of what God required.

These three parables are about the kingdom of God. The kingdom is one in which a forgiving father offers people a chance to return to him. The Judaism of the Pharisees and Scribes did not care for the lost.

The meaning of the parables for today

Christians see, in the three parables of the lost, a picture of God's forgiveness. He does not hold sin against people.

They also claim that forgiveness produces reconciliation only when it is preceded by repentance. God forgives without conditions, but forgiveness is only effective when, like the younger son, a person realises the need to be forgiven.

The Parable of the Pharisee and the Tax-collector (18:9–14)

The understanding of this parable hinges on the extreme contrast made between the two characters, the Pharisee and the Tax-collector.

THE PHARISEE	THE TAX-COLLECTOR
Made people aware of his presence by standing up in full view of everybody in the Temple;	Stood at the back of the Temple, his eyes downcast;
Boasted to God about his goodness in fasting and giving of tithes;	Confessed his failings to God and acknowledged the fact that he was a sinner;
Belittled, sarcastically, all who were not like him, especially the tax-collector	Refrained from any criticism of others.

The Pharisees's words are not even a prayer. They are merely arrogant words in praise of himself. In contrast the tax-collector shows true humility as he comes to God in prayer. He is the one who is reconciled to God.

Meaning
The parable is teaching that prayer must be offered with the right spirit. This spirit must be one of humility that recognises dependence on God. In this way reconciliation to God can take place.

The meaning of the parable for today

Christians would claim that this parable is at the very heart of the meaning of prayer. There is no place for boastfulness before God. Prayer must be approached in the right spirit of humility.

Study Skills

Knowledge

1   What is a parable?
2   What is an allegory?
3   In the Parable of the Wineskins what does Jesus advise not to do with new wine?
4   List the four types of ground mentioned in the Parable of the Sower. What happened to the seed in each case?
5   In the Parable of the Lamp, where does Jesus say the lamp should not be put?
6   In the Parable of the Wedding Guests, what did Jesus advise his hearers to do when invited to a wedding?
7   In the Parable of the Great Banquet, what excuses did the invited guests give for not accepting their invitations?
8   Which two sorts of people did the master of the house invite instead?
9   In the Parable of the Lost Son, how did the younger son squander his money?
10   When did he come to his senses?
11   In the Parable of the Pharisee and the tax-collector, what was the difference between the two in their attitudes to prayer?

Understanding

12   What might Jesus have meant by the Parable of the Sower when he first told it? Explain the allegorical meaning that is given in Luke's Gospel.
13   What do you understand to be the message of repentance and forgiveness found in the parables in Luke's Gospel?

Evaluation

14   What do you think is the significance of the three main characters in the parable of the Lost Son for Christians today?

The Claims of the Kingdom

The Parable of the Good Samaritan (10:25–37)

This parable arises from a question asked of Jesus by a

lawyer who was trying to test Jesus. The original question the lawyer asked was

> Master, what must I do to inherit eternal life? (10:25).

Jesus answered by asking a question in return. He asked the lawyer to tell him what the Law said. The lawyer made a good reply. To win eternal life one must love God and love your neighbour. He was congratulated on his answer by Jesus.

The lawyer, however, still wished to win his argument and asked a second question,

> Who is my neighbour?

Jesus replied with the Parable of the Good Samaritan.

A man on his way to Jericho was attacked, robbed and left for dead. Both the Priest and Levite went by without helping him. It was not that they were insensitive or evil men. The Law prevented them from helping. To touch a dead man or to come into contact with the blood of an injured person would make them unclean and mean that they could not carry out their duties. They put the claims of the Law first. The Samaritan stopped, helped and rescued the unfortunate traveller.

The parable concludes with Jesus making the lawyer admit that the Samaritan had been the good neighbour.

Meaning

The answer of the lawyer to the question of Jesus about what the Law said deserved the congratulations of Jesus. The two great principles of the kingdom of God are to love God and to love one's neighbour. The parable itself has a clear single meaning. If obedience to the Law takes precedence over human need then there is something wrong with the Law. The true definition of neighbour is anyone in need, irrespective of religious, racial, social or any other division.

The meaning of the parable for today

Christians see, in this parable, the command to treat every individual human being as a neighbour. There can be no room for prejudice in dealing with people. It is true that history records frequent occasions when this has been forgotten and prejudice has shown itself in religious, racial and class distinctions. Christians would claim this is totally foreign to true Christianity. The claims of the kingdom of God dictate that all people must be treated the same and held in the same esteem.

The Friend at Midnight (11:5–13) & The Unjust Judge (18:1–8)

These two parables are similar in theme. The first is about a person who had a friend who woke him up in the middle of the night to borrow some food because he had just received an unexpected visitor. At first the man was reluctant to help but in the end does so, not out of friendship, but because of the persistence of his neighbour.

The second story is about a heartless judge who grants a poor widow's appeal, not because he cared, nor because he wished to do his job properly, but simply to keep the nagging woman quiet.

Meaning
The meaning of these two parables is the same. It is not that God is reluctant to answer prayer unless he is pestered. It is that God is willing to answer those who persist in prayer. He is not like the friend at midnight or the unjust judge. He will respond.

The meaning of the parable for today

Most Christians consider prayer to be important, as it is through prayer that the relationship with God can mature. They accept the teaching of Jesus:

> Ask, and you will receive; seek, and you will find; knock, and the door will be opened. For everyone who asks receives, he who seeks finds, and to him who knocks, the door will be opened (11:9–10).

Some people claim that this is a false promise and that they have asked God but no answer has been given. Most Christians would realise that there are three answers to prayer; 'Yes'; 'No'; or 'Not yet'. They are confident to leave all in God's hands, knowing that he will not let them down. Even most human fathers, however evil, do not ill treat their children. So God, who is perfect, will answer all prayers in the way that is best for his children (11:11–13).

The Crafty Steward (16:1–8)

This is, without doubt, the most difficult parable in Luke's Gospel. It tells the story of a dishonest steward who is called to give an account of his master's business prior to being dismissed. The steward, worried about his future unemployment, makes friends with those who are in debt to his master by wiping out a proportion of their debts. He is commended for his astute actions by his master.

Meaning

Jesus stresses that those who belong to his kingdom need to be no less shrewd or astute than the rest of humanity. Some scholars claim that any temptation to allegorise this parable must be resisted for all the characters are dishonest and consistent in their dishonesty.

1 The rich man is himself dishonest because he appointed a steward whom he commended for actions which were in themselves dishonest.
2 The steward had not only cheated his master but goes on cheating him in order to acquire some friends and so protect himself from the probable consequences of his dishonest dealings.
3 The debtors are dishonest because they co-operate with the steward in defrauding the master and also, in all probability, in being prepared to give sanctuary to the thief.

Other scholars suggest that the parable is not as simple as this. The steward had squandered his master's property. What the steward had done had not actually harmed his master but he had charged a high rate of interest on loans, so that he could pocket the difference. In view of the threat of dismissal, the steward decided to give up his easy profits and earn the friendship of his master's debtors by asking them to pay off the loan with little or no interest at all.

The second interpretation at least makes sense of the master's comment that the steward is to be praised for his astuteness. The master had not been cheated of his goods in the end and had, in fact, recovered his invested capital. In the time of crisis, in which the steward had found himself, he had acted honestly.

The meaning of the parable for today

The meaning of this parable for Christians today is that in all dealings with people, the claim of Christianity is to act honestly. There is no room for dishonesty, cheating or selfishness. If that honesty wins friends then that is all to the good.

The Crisis of the Kingdom

GENERAL NOTE ON THE PARABLES OF CRISIS

- These parables must be understood in the context of the crisis facing the nation.
- Jesus realised that the failure of the Jews to accept that the kingdom of God had arrived would lead to an inevitable crisis.
- Their rejection of the Messiah would also accelerate the time of crisis.
- The crisis was twofold:

  1   The immediate crisis was the coming destruction of Jerusalem by the Romans in 70 AD (which, in all probability had happened, by the time Luke writes his Gospel).
  2   The long-term crisis was that Jesus would, after his resurrection, return to establish the rule of God on earth and this would involve judgment of those who had rejected him.

- The parables in this section deal with both the immediate crisis and the crisis to come at the end of the age.

The Parables of the Rich Fool (12:13–21); The Watchful Servants (12:35–38); The Burglar (12:39); and the Faithful and Unfaithful Servants (12:42–46)

Luke groups together these four parables which follow a similar theme.

1   On one occasion, Jesus is surrounded by a large crowd. A man asks Jesus to tell his brother to divide the property between them. It was quite common in Judaism for an appeal to be made to a religious leader in matters of legal inheritance. Jesus refused the role of arbitrator. Instead he gave two warnings:

To the poor he said:

Be on your guard against greed of every kind.

To the rich he said:

wealth does not give. . . life (12:15).

Then Jesus went on to tell the Parable of the Rich Man who hoarded his possessions to make sure his future was secure. He retired to enjoy his life. He told himself he could take life easy

eat, drink, and enjoy yourself (12:19).

That night he died and was parted from his wealth.

2 The Parable of the Watchful Servants is a simple story that tells of the servants who were ready for their master's return from a wedding.

3 The Parable of the Burglar states simply that if the householder knew what time the burglar was to arrive, he would prevent the burglary taking place.

4 The Parable of the Faithful and Unfaithful steward is a story of contrasts. It is very similar to the story of the watchful servants. This time, however, the contrast is drawn between the faithful servant who was ready for his master's return and the unfaithful one who spent his time bullying the other servants and getting drunk.

Meaning
There are two basic meanings to be found in these parables.

1 In the Parable of the Rich Fool there is a warning against greed. Wealth does not restore a person to God.
2 Originally this parable and the other three were stories which warned against the coming catastrophe of the end, when a person may be faced with either personal death or the end of the world. The early Church saw, in these parables, a warning to be faithful in the interim period prior to the Second Coming. They thought the day of God's judgment was near when an account would be required of their stewardship.

The meaning of the parable for today

Both these meanings are seen as important to Christians today. Many would claim that the teaching of Jesus is still relevant and that it is virtually impossible to be totally committed to amassing wealth and serve God at the same time. Many Christians also see life as an important preparation for death. They see eternity in terms of the response made to God while on earth. In addition to this, no one can forecast the moment of death. It can come at the least expected time, as indeed, can the end of the world and the Second Coming of Jesus.

The Barren Fig Tree (13:6–9)

This is the story of a man, who noticed that his fig tree had not produced any fruit for three years. He was all for cutting the tree down but was prevented from doing so by the gardener, who requested one more year in which the tree could be nurtured. If that did not work then the tree should be cut down.

Meaning
The fig tree stood for Israel. Jesus had come in search of the fruit of response to God. He had found little response. Israel's time for repentance was short. This was their last chance.

The early Church would have applied this parable to the fate of Jerusalem. The city was destroyed in AD 70 and the belief, at the time, was that the reason for this destruction was the lack of response to the message of God through Jesus.

The meaning of the parable for today

Many Christians today see, in this parable, the importance of repentance. Repentance means to turn around; to redirect life and return to God. It is a necessary part of being a Christian.

The Rich Man and Lazarus (16:19–31)

This parable is one of contrasts which can be seen throughout the story.

(a) In the first part of the parable, the contrast is made between the rich man and the poor man. The rich man was probably meant to be a Sadducee as they dressed

in purple and fine linen (*16:19*).

The poor man was in such a sorry state that the dogs

used to come and lick his sores (*16:21*).

Both die. The poor man went to heaven

to be with Abraham;

the rich man went to the underworld . . .

in Hades, where he was in torment.

(b) In the second part of the parable the contrast continues, though in reverse. Lazarus is now comforted while the rich man is in torment. The gulf between the two is final. The parable makes the point that there is an after-life which continues on from mortal life so that behaviour on earth has consequences for the next life.

(c) In the third part of the story, the rich man asks for Lazarus to be sent back to warn his brothers. He claims the message of scripture will not be enough to save them and requests a resurrection appearance. This is refused.

Meaning
The teaching of the parable can be summarised:

– Wealth must not be squandered selfishly.
– There is an after-life in which people are called to account.
– The resurrection does not make faith easier. It can never be regarded as proof.

The meaning of the parable for today

Many Christians point to this parable in discussing both the next life and also faith in the resurrection. The parable gives a clear indication that the state of life after death is in some way determined by actions during life on earth. They would not claim the parable holds the whole truth. There is no indication that all those who are poor naturally assume a place in heaven, nor that all the rich are condemned to hell. However, the way a person lives, in the sense of attitude to both God and other people seems to be taken into account. A person who is completely selfish and has little regard for people in need should not be surprised if this determines future life.

Secondly, Christians point to the importance of the truth that the resurrection cannot be proved. It is a matter of faith. After all, the prophecy at the end of the parable proved to be true:

they will pay no heed even if someone should rise from the dead (16:31).

The resurrection of Jesus did not mean that all men and women automatically believed. It remains a matter of faith.

The Parable of the Pounds (19:11–27)

There are two important matters to note regarding this parable before its meaning can be discovered:

1   v.11 is Luke's own comment on the parable. As far as he was concerned the parable is addressed to the disciples and through them the early Church. The call is one of faithfulness in the time before the second coming of Jesus.
2   Certain verses of the parable do not belong to the original story. They are:

> . . . to be appointed king and then return (19:12).

> His fellow-citizens hated him, and they sent a delegation on his heels to say, 'We do not want this man as our king'. However, back he came as king . . . (19:14–15).

> But as for those enemies of mine who did not want me for their king, bring them here and slaughter them in my presence (19:27).

The verses detract from the simplicity of the parable. They probably refer to Archelaus, one of the sons of Herod the Great, who after Herod's death in 4 BC, ruled over the region of Judaea. In 6 AD he went to Rome to try to persuade the Roman Emperor to give him the whole of his father's kingdom. This would have involved the removal of Herod Antipas from Galilee, and Philip, from the region of Ituraea and Trachonitis (3:1). The Jews sent a delegation to Rome to complain to the Emperor about Archelaus. As a result of all this political diplomacy, Archelaus was sacked by the Romans and sent into exile and Judaea became a province of Rome administered by a Procurator, the most famous being Pontius Pilate. The historical facts do not fit exactly the details recorded in the parable, as Archelaus did not return. Nevertheless, this is probably the event that stands behind the additions made to the parable.

   The parable, as recorded by Luke, is a little complicated, especially compared with the simplicity of Matthew's version (Matthew 25:14–30). There are ten servants, who are given a pound each, but when the king returns, only three of the servants report back. The first two have been successful and are rewarded; the third had failed and is punished.

Meaning
The parable has two meanings:

1   Originally, it was most probably directed against the
    Scribes and Pharisees, who like the third servant, had
    kept the message of God to themselves with their
    exclusiveness. Considering themselves to be superior, they
    cared little for the ordinary person and looked down on
    the sinners.
2   By the time Luke writes his Gospel, the meaning of the
    parable had changed. The early Church used it as a call to
    faithfulness and obedience in the interim time before the
    second coming of Jesus.

The meaning of the parable for today

Many Christians see, in this parable, the command to use the
talents and abilities they have been given in the service of God
and all people. They must not keep such gifts to themselves.

They would admit that this is a very modern interpretation of
the parable and that the original meanings of faithfulness and
obedience, care and concern for others, are still fundamental to
Christian teaching today.

The Parable of the Wicked Husbandmen (20:9–19)

This is one of the best examples of allegory in the Gospels.
The parable is based on Isaiah 5:1–7 where there is an Old
Testament 'parable' about a vineyard that yielded only wild
grapes. This signified the faithlessness of Israel.

Meaning
This allegory has obviously been developed in the period of
the Oral Tradition by the early Church to show what is
known as 'Salvation History'. Salvation history is the story of
God and his people and how God, since creation, has
attempted to reconcile them to himself.

The allegory is easily understood using the following key:

The owner of the Vineyard ....God
The vineyard ....Israel
The tenants ....Jewish Leaders
The servants ....The prophets
The son ....Jesus
The killing of the son ....The crucifixion

Others ....Gentiles
The stone ....The resurrection of Jesus

Verses 17–18 are not part of the original story. It is a saying used by the early Church to indicate the resurrection. Jesus, rejected by the Jews, rises to become the keystone of the faith. It was included here to complete the full story of salvation history, for to end with the killing of the son would have been incomplete.

Jesus' audience, however, would not have recognised the 'son' as Jesus because they would not have realised that he was going to die. There must be, therefore, another meaning of the parable before it was developed into the allegory.

The parable is a true-to-life description of a Galilean peasant's attitude towards the foreign landlords, of which there were many. This parable may refer to the fact that in Jesus' time the Zealots (this was the name given to nationalists) were stirring up the peasants to revolt against such landlords.

The fact that the owner of the vineyard is living abroad is the key to understanding the parable. The tenants take liberties with the messengers because they know the owner is far away. The son's arrival makes the tenants assume the owner is dead and that the son has come to claim his inheritance.

According to Jewish law, if the property became ownerless then it would become the property of the tenants. So they kill the son to acquire the vineyard.

The parable shows the depths to which the tenants will sink. Perhaps Jesus is telling this parable against the Jewish leaders who, in their self-righteousness had not listened to God. They have rejected both God and his messengers. So the vineyard will be given to others. Perhaps Jesus meant by this the 'outcasts' of Jewish society, although it is equally possible that he meant that God's message of the kingdom was for everyone regardless of race.

The meaning of the parable for today

Jesus came to call all people to return to God. His own people, the Jews, rejected him. In the earliest period of Christianity the church was very much influenced by Jewish culture and religion. With the conversion and work of St Paul and his friends, however, the church moved out and spread throughout the Roman Empire.

The vineyard was given to others;

to the Gentiles.

The allegory of the wicked husbandmen remains for Christians today the most superb summary of God's plan for the human race. They believe that God created the world and chose the Jews to be his tenants. They were to look after the vineyard of creation. From time to time they strayed away from God. He sent messages through the prophets calling for them to return to him. These were largely ignored. In the end he sent his son to make a final appeal for them to return to him. His son was rejected, and put to death. But God refused to accept this rejection and raised Jesus from the dead. This death and resurrection of Jesus was for all men and women, not just the Jews, so that all might believe in him and through him, be reconciled to God.

Study Skills

Knowledge

1 Which parable did Jesus tell in response to the question 'Master, what must I do to inherit eternal life?'
2 Who were the two characters who 'went by on the other side' in the Parable of the Good Samaritan?
3 Why does the man finally answer his friend's request in the Parable of the Friend at Midnight?
4 How did the crafty steward try to obtain some friends when threatened with unemployment?
5 What did God say to the man in the Parable of the Rich Fool?
6 Why did the owner of the fig tree want to cut it down?
7 Give a careful account of the Parable of the Rich Man and Lazarus?
8 What did the third servant do with the pound given to him by the noble man in the Parable of the Pounds?
9 What does the vineyard represent in the Parable of the Wicked Husbandmen?
10 How is the resurrection included in the allegorical interpretation of this parable?

Understanding

11 What do you understand by the phrase 'the kingdom of God'? Explain how the parables show that this kingdom is both present and future.

12 Explain the meaning of:

(a) the Parable of the Rich Fool
(b) the Parable of the Rich Man and Lazarus
(c) the Parable of the Wicked Husbandmen?

Evaluation

13 Do you think it is easier to understand parables or allegories? Illustrate your answer with examples from Luke's Gospel.

14 Write a modern parable showing one aspect of the kingdom of God for today.

Examination Practice

Describe briefly the Parable of the Good Samaritan.   (4)
What do you think Jesus is teaching in this parable, apart
from the truth that all people are neighbours?   (4)
Name two parables in Luke which use the image of a seed or
seeds   (4)
Some people would claim that the parables are out-of-date
and have little to say to a modern world. What are your views?
Give reasons for your answer.   (6)
All the parables in Luke teach about different aspects of the
same subject. What is it?

(2)

Practical Work

• Design a poster or collage showing the parables of Luke's Gospel and their meanings. Highlight the four different aspects of the teaching of the parables about the kingdom of God.

5 The Miracles of Jesus in Luke's Gospel

The purpose of this chapter is to examine the miracle stories found in Luke's Gospel. It is important, however, first of all to look at some questions regarding the approach to this subject.
– What is a miracle?
– Did Jesus perform miracles?
– Why did Jesus heal people?
– The relationship between faith and miracle
– What is faith?
– The Church and healing today
– Exorcisms
– The healing miracles
– The raising from the dead miracles
– Nature miracles

What is a miracle?

In the twentieth century a miracle is thought of as something extra-ordinary. It is seen as a direct intervention by God that breaks all the normal laws of nature. It is something that cannot be explained away. Because of this modern definition of miracles many people seem to think miracles do not happen very often today. They are regarded as belonging to an earlier age of superstition and ignorance.

The real meaning of the miracles will be missed if they are treated simply as 'newspaper reports'. The miracles are something much more important. They express the belief that the early Christians had in and about Jesus.

It must be remembered that the Gospel is an expression of Christian belief. Some Christians would say the Gospel is not the source or proof of what happened. So with regard to the miracles, questions such as, 'Could this happen?' or 'What happened?' are not the questions to ask. The questions that must be asked about the miracles are:

1   Why did the Gospel writers include these stories?

2   What did these stories mean to them?
3   Do these stories have any importance for Christians today?

Did Jesus perform Miracles?

There is little doubt that Jesus performed many miracles during his ministry. He is even accused of casting out devils by the power of Satan (11:15). Such an accusation is hardly likely to have been invented by either the disciples or his enemies if he had been unable to cast out evil spirits.

Many scholars, however, would doubt whether the accounts in the Gospels are the reports of actual occurrences. In keeping with all the material of the Gospel, the miracle accounts have gone through two separate periods of development. The first is the period of oral tradition when the stories of Jesus were used and passed on by the Church. The second is the influence of the Gospel writers themselves.

As a result of these developments it is possible to make three claims regarding the miracles in Luke's Gospel.

1   It is impossible to discover the actual occurrence that stands behind the individual accounts.
2   The accounts, even if they are based on genuine memory, as many undoubtedly are, are more examples of the kind of thing Jesus used to do.
3   All the miracles of healing follow a set pattern:
    (a) Setting: description of illness, etc.;
    (b) Cure: by command, touch, at a distance.
    (c) Crowd response: the reaction of the onlookers.

WHY THE STORY WAS REMEMBERED

- The early Church used the miracles to express the belief that God is working among people through the Messiah.
- In this way the miracles show the developing faith of the early Church.
- This development is the result of using the miracle stories in preaching and teaching.

Why did Jesus Heal People?

Many people would say that Jesus could not help himself healing people because of his overwhelming feeling of compassion and love for them. Certainly Christians believe that compassion and love are qualities that Jesus possessed.

It should be noted, however, that there is only one miracle in Luke's Gospel where it states that Jesus healed out of a sense of compassion or pity (7:13).

The answer to the question, 'Why did Jesus heal?' can be found in one of the miracles itself. The woman who had a haemorrhage for twelve years and probably suffered from haemophilia, touched the cloak of Jesus believing that was all she had to do to be healed. Jesus said to her,

> My daughter, your faith has cured you. Go in peace (8:47).

The older translations have at this point the words: 'Your faith has made you whole.' Jesus wished people to be 'whole', in body, mind and spirit.

This is the real reason for the miracles of healing, to bring a wholeness of life to those in need.

The Relationship between Faith and Miracle

It is important, however, to understand exactly what the connection is between the faith and miracle. Unfortunately, many people today see the miracles as events that make people believe. It is as if they are saying, 'We believe in Jesus because he proved who he was by working miracles'. The reverse is also true. Some people do not believe in Jesus because they do not believe in the miracles. They misunderstand the purpose of the miracles in thinking they are meant to bring about faith. Such people seem to connect miracle and faith like this:

thinking they are meant to bring about faith. Such people seem to connect miracle and faith like this:

$$MIRACLE \rightarrow leading\ to \rightarrow FAITH$$

This idea is not the one found in Luke's Gospel. It is not what the Christian believes. The Christian believes in Jesus because of the resurrection, not because he performed miracles. The early Christians believed in him because they thought he was alive and with them. It has been the same for Christians throughout history. The connection between miracles and faith is quite simple. It is the opposite of what a lot of people think today. Faith comes before the miracle. The connection between faith and miracle is:

$$FAITH \rightarrow leading\ to \rightarrow MIRACLE$$

What is Faith?

Once again, this needs to be clearly stated. Many people seem to have an understanding of faith which borders on superstition. To them Jesus is someone with special powers, almost like an hypnotist, who could place inside a person the belief that they could be healed and therefore show faith.

Such a viewpoint is not found in the miracles of the Gospel. Some of the miracles are, for example, performed 'at a distance' where no such psychological relationship could possibly exist (e.g. The Centurion's Servant 7:1–10). In the Gospel, faith is seen as an act of trust by which a person relies not on himself but on Jesus. It is an energetic seeking after the power of God. It is the firm belief that he can do something for them through Jesus.

Faith has two main characteristics:

1   it is an *active faith*; a belief that something needs to be done and can be done by this man Jesus. This belief shows itself in action:
    e.g. The cure of the paralysed man (5:17–26)
2   It is a *praying faith*; in the sense of a plea or request; faith that believes to ask is to receive.
    e.g. The cure of the leper (5:12–16)

Faith is the request and miracle is the answer. It is always in that order.

The Church and healing today

The Christian Church still practises healing. Sometimes it is by praying over the sick person. At other times it may be by anointing the sick person with oil. The Church does this because the will of Jesus is that all people should be whole in body, mind and spirit. A person with faith prays for healing in the belief that healing can take place. Sometimes a sick person's friends show their faith in action such as taking a person to a healing service or to some centre of healing such as Lourdes. Faith coming before and bringing about healing is as real to many Christians today as it was at the time of the Gospel.

The miracle stories in Luke's Gospel can be divided into four main sections:

1 Exorcisms
2 Healing miracles
3 Raising from the dead
4 Nature miracles

Exorcisms

1 The Capernaum demoniac 4:31–37
2 The Gergesene demoniac 8:26–39
3 The epileptic boy 9:37–43

Healing Miracles

I Healing on the Sabbath
4 Simon's mother-in-law 4:38–39
5 The man with the withered arm 6:6–11
    The enfeebled woman 13:10–17
    The man with dropsy 14:1–6

II Healing Miracles Showing Faith
6 The leper 5:12–16 and the ten lepers 17:11–19
7 The paralysed man 5:17–26
8 The Centurion's servant 7:1–10
9 The woman with the haemorrhage 8:43–48
10 The blind man at Jericho 18:35–43

Raising from the Dead

11   The widow of Nain's son.................................... 7:11–17
12   The raising of Jairus' daughter 8:40–42, 49–56

Nature Miracles

13   The calming of the storm 8:22–25
14   The feeding of the five thousand 9:10–17

Exorcisms

1 The Capernaum Demoniac (4:31–37)

An exorcism is the casting out of an evil spirit from a person.

The first miracle recorded by Luke is the casting out of an evil spirit by a direct command.

> 'Be silent', he said, 'and come out of him' (4:35).

Jesus faces evil and by the authority he has, commands the evil spirits to go and they flee.

Why the Story was Remembered
This miracle is remembered by the early Church because it contains the title 'Holy One of God'. The evil spirits recognised Jesus. That is why they called out

> What do you want with us . . . Have you come to destroy us? (4:34).

The title 'Holy One of God' is found only in this story. It is a Messianic title. It means that Jesus is seen as belonging to God in a special way. He is Messiah (see Chapter 9).

The evil spirit says 'Have you come to destroy us?' This suggests that there was more than one. Perhaps this one representative speaks for all the evil spirits. They are all faced with the power of God in Jesus who has come to destroy them.

Luke's Use of the Story
Luke states that all the people were astonished as they witnessed this contest between good and evil.

Luke claims that this is because of the *authority* of Jesus.

> He gives orders ... with authority and power, and
> out they go (4:36).

This authority comes from God.

Jesus also taught the people with *power*. This is a word
used by Luke to indicate that Jesus was filled with the Holy
Spirit. The miracle is set by Luke just after Jesus is

(a) baptised with the Spirit at his baptism (3:21–22);
(b) led by the Spirit into the wilderness to face the
temptations (4:1);
(c) 'anointed' with the Spirit in the synagogue at
Nazareth (4:14–30).

So Jesus now teaches by the power of the Spirit.

2   The Gergesene Demoniac (8:26–39)

The place where this exorcism took place differs according to
the various translations of the Gospel. There are three
alternatives; Gerasene, Gergesene or Gadarene. They are all
intended to be the same place, in Gentile country across the
Sea of Galilee.

The symptoms of being possessed by an evil spirit are
described in detail; an interest in death; abnormal physical
strength, insensitivity to pain and the refusal to wear clothes.

Why the Story was Remembered
The man was possessed by many devils. His name is Legion.
A Roman legion consisted of 6000 men. Legion was very
strong. For his own safety he was often chained up, but he
was able to break free. Yet soon afterwards he sat at the feet
of Jesus

> clothed and in his right mind (8:35).

Once again evil is powerless when faced with God acting
through Jesus.

The miracle was remembered by the early Church because
it uses another rare Messianic title;

> Son of the Most High God.

Jesus, as Messiah, is the 'Son of the Most High God' and as
such has power over evil.

One strange feature of the account is the conversation
between Jesus and Legion. The evil spirits asked to go into
the pigs that were nearby. They were given permission and
were destroyed as the herd of pigs drowned in the lake.

What the early Church believed about this is quite clear. Jesus was concerned to free a human life from the power of Satan at whatever the cost. One human life was more important than a whole herd of pigs.

Luke's Use of the Story
It is interesting that the story of Legion ends on a note of discipleship. Legion wished to be a disciple but Jesus told him to remain where he was in his own district and tell all the people what

> God has done for you (8:39).

Again the action of Jesus is seen by Luke as the action of God. In this sense Legion was the first missionary figure in the Gospel. This fits in with Luke's great emphasis on universalism. Jesus had come to save everybody, regardless of race.

A DIFFICULTY

Some Christians today have a difficulty with this story. Jesus seemed to have no respect for the livelihood of a Gentile pig farmer. He allowed the herd of pigs to be destroyed.

There are three ways of explaining the difficulty:

1   The first is to accept it as being a contest between good and evil. (See above)
2   The second is to treat the death of the pigs as a coincidence. It has nothing at all to do with the cure of Legion.
3   The third is to say that the death of the pigs did not take place on the same occasion at all and has nothing to do with the miracle. It only became connected with the miracle because both events took place in the same village.

---

3   The Epileptic Boy (9:37–43)

Although the Apostles had been successful in casting out evil spirits on their missionary tour (9:1ff) they could not help in this case. The symptoms described in this account seem to show some form of epilepsy.

Why the Story was Remembered
It is difficult to decide to whom Jesus is speaking when he says,

> What an unbelieving and perverse generation! How long shall I be with you and endure you all? (9:41).

In the Markan account of the same story it is obvious that Jesus is talking to his disciples but it would seem that Luke directs the sentence to the father. Perhaps Luke is trying to point out the necessity of faith which seems to be lacking in the father.

It would make more sense, however, for Jesus to be addressing the Apostles, as he goes on to say that their own period of testing is coming (9:44–45).

Once again, through faith Jesus was able to defeat Satan. This miracle was important to the early Church because it encouraged them in situations where faith was being tested.

Luke's Use of the Story
Luke uses this story to make a comment on the person of Jesus. The contrast is drawn between the Apostles, who could not cast the evil spirit out of the boy, and Jesus, who rebuked the spirit and cured the boy. Luke has added the last sentence which shows what he thinks of Jesus.

> they were all struck with awe at the majesty of God (9:43).

In other words, Jesus acts as God and defeats evil.

The message of the exorcisms for today

Our twentieth century idea of illness is different from that of New Testament times. Most illness has a physical cause with physical symptoms. At the time of Jesus these symptoms may have been recognised but the cause would have been unknown. Some exorcisms, for example, describe conditions which today would be thought of as mental illness or in some cases, epilepsy. There is no suggestion that Christians today view mental illness or epilepsy as the result of being possessed by evil.

It would be foolish, however, to dismiss evil altogether. Many Christians believe it is possible for a person to be possessed by a force contrary to good; a force called evil.

Study Skills

Knowledge

1   What is an exorcism?
2   Give an example of 'active' faith.
3   Give an example of 'praying' faith.
4   What did the man with the unclean spirit in the synagogue at Capernaum cry out?
5   How does Luke describe Legion's appearance and character?
6   What did Jesus tell Legion to do?
7   In which miracle is Jesus called 'Holy One of God'?
8   Give a brief account of the healing of the epileptic boy.

Understanding

9   What do you understand to be the relationship between faith and miracle?
10   How does our understanding of illness today differ from that at the time of Jesus? Describe, briefly, two miracles that illustrate this difference.

Evaluation

11   Why do you think that people at the time of Jesus thought that mental illness was caused by demonic possession? Do people still believe in possession by evil today?
12   Why do you think the miracles of exorcism were remembered by the early Church and recorded by Luke?

Healing Miracles:
I   Healing on the Sabbath
4 Simon's Mother-in-law (4:38–39)

This is a simple healing miracle which has no real meaning for us other than that the sufferer is ill. It happened on the Sabbath but does not cause any controversy. It does not conform to the usual miracle pattern. It does not show the importance of faith.

Perhaps the only reason it forms part of the Christian tradition is that it is Simon's mother-in-law. The Simon mentioned was most probably the Apostle Peter. Peter was a nickname given to Simon by Jesus (Matthew 16:17–18). Peter (in Greek, 'Petros') means a rock. It seems natural that it would be remembered by Simon Peter and passed on.

5 The Man with the Withered Arm (6:6–11)
The Enfeebled·Woman (13:10–17)
The Man with Dropsy (14:1–6)

The keeping of the Sabbath was extremely important to the survival of the Jewish religion. The book of Genesis tells how God had created the world in six days and commanded the seventh to be a day of rest. No work could be done on the Sabbath. Any threat to the Sabbath day was seen as a threat to the Jewish faith as a whole. Such a threat was bound to meet with opposition.

The Jewish law stated that no healing could take place on the Sabbath day unless it was a matter of life and death. Any non-emergency must wait until the Sabbath was over.

Luke records three miracles on the theme of healing on the Sabbath; a man with the withered arm; an enfeebled woman; and a man with dropsy. Some scholars think that all three belong to the same basic source, or at the very least two sources. Certainly they contain similar sayings and illustrations as can be seen below.

In these three miracles Jesus claimed the right to do any action on the Sabbath that was for the good of people. To heal on the Sabbath was part of that claim.

There is no mention of faith because faith is not an important truth in this narrative. What is important is that Jesus saw that blind obedience to the letter of the law was stopping a man from being healed.

Why the Stories were Remembered
The Church remembered these miracles for two reasons:

(i) The great pronouncement of Jesus found in full in the cure of the man with the withered arm and repeated in abbreviated form in the healing of the man with dropsy:

> Is it permitted to do good or to do evil on the
> Sabbath, to save life or to destroy it? (*6:9; 14:3*).

'To do good' and 'to save life' are both seen as the actions of God. The well-known phrase 'Jesus went about doing good' does not mean that Jesus was just a good man doing good deeds. It means that he was acting as the Messiah for 'to do good' is a Messianic action. As Messiah Jesus is above the Jewish Law (2:28).

	Withered Arm	**Enfeebled Woman**	**Dropsical Man**
Where?	Synagogue	Synagogue	House of Pharisee
Who was watching?	Lawyers and Pharisees	President of the Synagogue	Lawyers and Pharisees
What did Jesus say to them?	'Is it permitted to do good or to do evil on the Sabbath, to save life or to destroy it?'		'Is it permitted to cure people on the Sabbath or not?'
The cure	'Stretch out your arm'. His arm was restored	'You are rid of your trouble'	He took the man and cured him
Reaction	They were angry	He was indignant	They said nothing
What did he/ they say/do?	Discussed what to do about Jesus	There are six working days. Cure then not on the Sabbath	
What Jesus said		'Hypocrites. Each of you takes ox or donkey for water on the Sabbath. Was it wrong to cure the woman?'	'If a donkey or ox falls into a well on Sabbath, do you not rescue it?'
Final reaction		Opponents confused. People overjoyed	They could find no reply

(ii)   The cure of the enfeebled woman and the healing of the man with dropsy both contain the clearest evidence against the taking of the Sabbath law too far. If an animal could be looked after or rescued on the Sabbath day, then it would seem somewhat strange that a person in need could not be helped. Jesus pointed out that taking the law this far was not in the interest of people.

Luke's Use of the Stories
The fact that Luke emphasises this point of healing on the Sabbath by including three miracles, all of which teach the same point, indicates that he was concerned that the message of Jesus' concern for the sick, under-privileged and the

outcast should be unquestionable. It is a major theme of Luke's Gospel.

The message of the miracles for today

The message of these miracles is a simple one. Most Christians believe that the need of an individual person is more important than any slavish observance of religious law.

Just as in Jesus' time, concern for the sick, under-privileged, outcast and those without rights or oppressed should be unquestionable.

II Healing Miracles Showing Faith

6 The Leper (5:12–16) and the Ten Lepers (17:11–19)

Luke includes two miracles concerning lepers. The first is taken from Mark's Gospel and involves the cure of a single leper; the second is from his own source and is a story about ten lepers. Many scholars believe that the story of the ten lepers is a development of the miracle of the one leper. There are similarities although the emphasis of the second miracle is different.

The details of the cure of the single leper are few. The place is unknown, as is the man's name. There do not seem to be any witnesses to the miracle. All that is recorded is a meeting between Jesus and a leper.

The second miracle takes place on the border between Galilee and Samaria (17:11). Jesus is confronted with ten lepers who request his help.

At the time of Jesus, the term 'leprosy' covered many skin complaints (see Leviticus 13), not just the disease known as leprosy today. In one sense the Jewish law was sensible in its attempt to stop the spread of contagious disease.

Why the Stories were Remembered
Both miracles are remembered because of the emphasis on faith. The leper has a 'praying faith' which expresses itself in a plea or request.

> If only you will you can cleanse me (5:12).

The ten lepers make a similar request. They stand at a distance and call to Jesus,

> Jesus, master, take pity on us (17:13).

In the first account Jesus gives an immediate answer,

> ... Jesus stretched out his hand, touched him, and said, 'Indeed I will; be clean again.' (5:13).

Jesus told the leper to go and show himself to the priest and make an offering for his healing. This was the law. The priest was the only one who could declare a person to be healed from their leprosy.

In the second account, Jesus told them to go and show themselves to the priests and while they were on their way, they discovered they were cured.

In both cases their faith in Jesus had produced healing.

Luke's Use of the Story
The miracle of the single leper is used in two ways:

1 Jesus is seen as fulfilling the Old Testament in the sense that he is greater than the Jewish Law. Illnesses such as leprosy are against God's will and must be defeated.
2 The account is set in a section of the Gospel that shows Jesus' authority. This authority is God given. Jesus is the representative of God.

The emphasis is changed in the second story. The climax of the account is the fact that one of the ten who was cured returns to Jesus to thank him (17:15). Luke makes the point that he was a Samaritan. Jesus asks what happened to the other nine.

> Could none be found to come back and give praise to God except this foreigner? (17:18).

The fact that the man was a Samaritan highlights the theme of universalism, a major theme of Luke's Gospel.

The message of the miracle for today

For Christians today, the curing of leprosy is not the most important thing about these miracles. The stories show the deeper truth that Jesus comes to people at the point of deepest need. The miracles express both the belief in a God who reaches out and 'touches'; a God who can heal and also the fact that not only healing but the whole message of Jesus is for all people.

7 The Paralysed Man (5:17–26)

Luke introduces this miracle with a sentence that must be exaggerated. It is doubtful if the audience consisted of people from every village in Galilee and from Judaea and even the capital Jerusalem. Luke intends there to be a wide audience for this miracle.

Originally this miracle was one of faith. The faith, shown by the friends of the paralysed man who carried the stretcher is an active faith. The details of how they opened up the roof and lowered the man down through the tiles to the feet of Jesus are so vivid that the account obviously has some true foundation to it. It is probably based on an eye-witness account.

There are, however, some difficulties with the miracle.

1 This is one of only two occasions in the Gospel where Jesus claims to forgive sins. The other occasion is at the anointing of Jesus by the sinful woman, and there the woman's sins had already been forgiven, even though Jesus tells her that her sins are forgiven (see Chapter 3).

2 The claim to forgive sins is supported by the miracle. Elsewhere in the Gospel Jesus avoids such claims and in the story of the Temptations Jesus resisted the idea of using miracles to prove who he was, or what he had come to do.

Why the Story was Remembered

Many scholars suggest that verses 20b–24a are not part of the original tradition from which this account is taken but are a very early addition by the Church. Such a suggestion makes sense when a comparison is made between the account with and without the addition. The account is complete and is a simple miracle of healing (see below).

The basic reasons for this suggestion are:

1 the early Church believed Jesus was the 'Son of Man' (see Chapter 3);

2 the early Church believed Jesus did forgive sins;

3 the early Church believed miracles were proof of who Jesus was; and

4 the early Church had to face the charge of blasphemy. This miracle showed that Jesus' claim to forgive sins was not blasphemous.

5:17 One day he was teaching, and Pharisees and teachers of the law were sitting round. People had come from every village of Galilee and from Judaea and Jerusalem, and the power of the Lord was with him to heal the sick. 18. Some men appeared carrying a paralysed man on a bed. They tried to bring him in and set him down in front of Jesus, 19. but finding no way to do so because of the crowd, they went up on to the roof and let him down through the tiling, bed and all, into the middle of the company in front of Jesus. 20. When Jesus saw their faith, he said, 24b. 'I say to you, stand up, take your bed, and go home.' 25. And at once he rose to his feet before their eyes, took up the bed he had been lying on, and went home praising God. 26. They were all lost in amazement and praised God; filled with awe they said, 'You would never believe the things we have seen today.'

20b. 'Man your sins are forgiven you.' 21. The lawyers and Pharisees began saying to themselves, 'who is this fellow with his blasphemous talk? Who but God alone can forgive sins?' 22. But Jesus knew what they were thinking and answered them: 'Why do you harbour thoughts like these? 23. Is it easier to say, "Your sins are forgiven you", or to say, "Stand up and walk"?' 24a. But to convince you that the Son of Man has the right on earth to forgive sins' – he turned to the paralysed man

. . .

Luke's use of the Story

Luke uses the story to show that Jesus does have the right to forgive sins. Luke is anxious to show, throughout his Gospel, compassion to the poor, sick and outcast. Forgiveness even plays a part in the crucifixion where Jesus forgives those who are crucifying him (23:34).

He can forgive sins because he has authority to do so and this authority comes from God.

The message of the miracle for today

Christians see, in this miracle, the eternal truth that sins can be forgiven and that this forgiveness comes through Jesus. Christians believe that the quality of forgiveness is most important in order to achieve not only personal closeness to God but reconciliation between people.

They believe Jesus died so that sins might be forgiven and therefore, this story is an illustration of this truth. Jesus forgives sins.

8 The Centurion's Servant (7:1–10)

This miracle is set in the town of Capernaum in Galilee. Living in Capernaum was a Roman centurion, who was obviously sympathetic to the Jews and their religion. It was he who had built the synagogue. At first it may seem surprising to find a Gentile so involved in Jewish affairs but it was not all that unusual. There were some Romans who did not believe in all their own pagan gods but who were inclined towards the idea of one universal God. This man had not become a Jew, probably because of his position within the Roman army. The centurion is also shown to be a compassionate man, for he cares about the health of one of his servants. He sent Jewish representatives to Jesus to ask him to help.

Why the Story was Remembered
This miracle was remembered for three reasons.

1 The healing of the servant was made possible by the prayerful faith of someone other than the sufferer. It is the centurion who has the faith that Jesus can do something.
2 The miracle was performed at a distance. Jesus does not meet the servant. What is even more amazing is that Jesus does not meet the centurion either. The centurion sent word to Jesus that it was not necessary for him to come in person. Jesus only had to say the word and he knew that the servant would be healed (7:7).
3 The centurion's faith is that Jesus' authority was from God. He explained, that as an officer in the army, he knew that his own commands would be obeyed without question because of his authority. In the same way, Jesus had authority which came from God (7:6–8).

Luke's Use of the Story
The centurion received, from Jesus, the highest praise given
to anyone in Luke's Gospel. He pronounces:

> I tell you, nowhere, even in Israel, have I found faith
> like this (7:9).

It should always be remembered that the man was a Gentile.
This Gentile had professed a faith that no Jew had, believing
Jesus had the authority and power to help. Luke uses this
story as the supreme example of his theme of universalism.
The Gospel was to be offered to Jew and Gentile alike.

The message of the miracle for today

*Christians believe that the good news of the message of Jesus is
for all people. It does not depend on race, colour, or class.
Everyone is the same in the eyes of God and his love, mercy and
forgiveness is for all. The grace of faith is offered to every
individual.*

9 The Woman with the Haemorrhage (8:43–48)

This miracle comes in the middle of the story of the raising
from the dead of Jairus' daughter. The woman, who was
probably suffering from haemophila, felt it was necessary to
approach Jesus secretly because her illness made her
'unclean' according to the Law. Jesus was aware of her touch
even though the crowd were pressing all around him. The
touch was the touch of faith. This is an unusual miracle. It is
the only one where someone touched Jesus believing that
was all they had to do to be healed. It is important not to
interpret the phrase that Jesus had felt some power go out of
him as though he were some sort of 'divine energy' source of
healing. The words simply mean that Jesus was conscious
that someone was seeking his help.

Why the Story was Remembered
It has already been stated that the miracle is important
because it gives the clearest reason why Jesus healed. His
wish was for a person to 'be made whole'.

Luke's Use of the Story
The Greek verb used in the phrase which is translated

> your faith has cured you . . . (8:48),

is the verb 'to save'. This verb is used in the Old Testament when it means the salvation of God for his people. The first readers of this Gospel would see, in the story of the woman with the haemorrhage, an illustration of the fact that the time of salvation has arrived in the person of Jesus. In him the Spirit of God is at work.

The message of the miracle for today

The wholeness of life is important to all Christians. They believe this to be God's will and that anything that hinders this is contrary to the will of God. Wholeness of body, mind and soul should be the prior concern of all Christians and they believe this wholeness can be found through faith.

10 The Blind Man at Jericho (18:35–43)

This is the last miracle in the Gospel. Jesus was on his way to Jerusalem and had reached Jericho. It is here that a blind beggar, sitting by the side of the road cried out to be cured of his blindness.

Why the Story is Remembered
The Church remembered this miracle because of the use of a rare title, 'Son of David'. This is a Messianic title. What the miracle is really saying is that the blind man considers Jesus to be Messiah.

Faith is shown in this miracle in the sense of a plea or request. The cry of the blind man,

> Jesus, Son of David, have pity on me (*18:38*)

shows a faith that persists even when he is told to be quiet by the crowd.

Luke's Use of the Story
There are two important matters to note about the use of this miracle.

> 1 your faith has cured you (*18:42*).

Once again Luke has used the Greek verb 'to save'. God's salvation is offered through Jesus.

> 2 he followed Jesus . . . (*18:43*).

The word 'disciple' in Greek means 'to follow'. The man became a disciple. This is the only miracle (with the possible exception of the Gergesene Demoniac) where the person healed is known to have become a disciple.

The message of the miracle for today

This miracle is the most complete of all miracles for in it is contained the outline of the Christian faith.

Through FAITH a person might come to understand and see in the sense of having INSIGHT. This leads to SALVATION and the result of salvation is DISCIPLESHIP.

FAITH is the INSIGHT
SALVATION is the RESULT
DISCIPLESHIP is the WAY

This is the experience of many Christians today. By faith they grow in understanding and insight. They draw near to God by the gift of his salvation and become disciples, following Jesus in their lives.

The Raising from the Dead Miracles

11 The Widow of Nain's Son (7:11–17)

This story has no mention of the requirement of faith. It seems to arise out of overwhelming compassion for the poor widow who was in the process of burying her only son.

When the Lord saw her his heart went out to her, and he said 'Weep no more' (*7:13*).

Why the Story was Remembered
Some scholars believe that this story is more theological than historical. It has overtones of an Old Testament story in which the prophet Elijah also raised a widow's son from death and 'gave him back to his mother' (7:15; 1 Kings 17:23). This reference to Elijah would have been fully understood by Jewish readers and would also account for the crowd response at the end of the story.

A great prophet has arisen among us. God has shown his care for his people (*7:16*).

Perhaps the story was remembered because:

(a)   it showed that Jesus has a lifegiving power no less powerful than that of Elijah before him.
(b)   More than this, it also indicated that Jesus was greater than Elijah. He is not just a prophet. In the next story in the Gospel, John the Baptist sent some disciples to Jesus to ask if

he was the one who was to come or should they begin to look elsewhere. The reply of Jesus states clearly that he is more than a prophet (7:22–23). He is Messiah.

Luke's Use of the Story

There can be no disputing the fact that Luke includes this story for one main reason. Jesus cannot only heal people but he can also conquer death. Death is the symbol of sin and evil but this is no longer a thing to be dreaded. The story is an expression of belief in the power of Jesus.

The message of the miracle for today

Christians still hold this same belief today. They believe that death has been conquered and that it is not the end of life. Many would also say that real life is only possible when one has accepted the finiteness of life on earth as something that God uses to draw people into a closer union with himself. This union is one in which there is no death, only eternal life.

12 The Raising of Jairus' Daughter (8:40–42; 49–56)

Jesus had just returned from the country of the Gergesenes. In the crowd that surrounded him was a man called Jairus, who was the president of one of the local synagogues.

Jairus pleaded with Jesus to cure his twelve-year-old daughter who was at home, dying. On the way Jesus cured the woman with the haemorrhage (see above).

Before they could arrive at Jairus' house, a message was received that the daughter had died. Jesus told Jairus not to worry but to have faith. He took Peter, James and John into the house where the girl was surrounded with people crying and wailing in their distress. When Jesus said the girl was only sleeping, they all laughed at him.

Jesus took the little girl by the hand and told her to get up. She got up immediately.

Why the Miracle was Remembered

Once again, faith is the key to this miracle. Jairus showed faith; a praying faith in asking Jesus to help. He believed help was possible from Jesus. When the message arrived that the child was dead, the message of Jesus was clear. This was a message not only to Jairus but to the whole Church.

Do not be afraid; only show faith (*8:50*).

Luke's Use of the Story
The main problem with this miracle is the question of whether or not Luke meant it as a healing or a raising from the dead miracle. Jesus said that the child was only asleep. Some people think that Jesus still meant death in the sense that it might be said today that a person had 'fallen asleep' when they had died. It must be noted, however, that Jesus made a point of saying that

> The child is not dead (8:52).

Whatever the interpretation, it is plain that both Luke and the early Church saw in this story an illustration of the power of God to raise the dead. The message of the miracle is that of a 'parable'. Death is not the end. Life comes after death.

The message of the miracle for today

As with the widow of Nain, the message of the miracle is that death is not the end. Jesus has power over death and new life comes after death.

Nature Miracles

Nature miracles are, for some people, the most difficult to accept.

1   They seem to be inconsistent with what is known of the laws of nature.
2   They are also inconsistent with the story of the Temptation of Jesus where he refused to use his powers to compel belief by spectacular 'proofs'.

They are, however, the only miracles performed without an audience other than the disciples. (Even the Feeding of the 5000 seems to pass unnoticed by the crowds. There is no 'crowd response' at all.) It would seem, therefore, that the nature miracles come from an early disciple source.

Whatever the original miracles were, there can be little doubt that the accounts, as recorded in the Gospel, have been developed from their first historical setting. They carry deeper theological meanings. This was done by the Church in the period of the oral tradition.

Luke has only two nature miracles.

11 The Calming of the Storm (8:22–25)

Sudden storms are quite common on the Sea of Galilee. They tend to subside as quickly as they arise. Standing behind this account is probably one such incident.

Why the Story was Remembered
Scholars tend to interpret this miracle as an 'allegory'. In the early days of the Church, Christians suffered persecution and had to have great faith to survive the violent opposition they received. This miracle shows a picture of the Church. The boat is the Church and the storm is the persecution of the Church. Those who lose heart and cry out in despair are reminded that Jesus is in command and he will steer the little ship of the Church into calmer waters. In the meantime they must keep their faith.

Luke's Use of the Story
In the Old Testament the sea was the symbol of chaos and evil, which could only be overcome by God. The question asked at the end of the miracle,

> who can this be? He gives his orders to wind and waves, and they obey him (*8:25*)

is left unanswered. The answer is obvious. Jesus, acting as God, is the one whom even wind and sea obey. The story is similar to the ideas found in the Old Testament.

> 'So they cried to the Lord in their trouble,
> and he brought them out of their distress.
> The storm sank to a murmur
> and the waves of the sea were stilled.
> They were glad then that all was calm,
> as he guided them to the harbour they desired'.
> (Psalm 107:29–30)

12 The Feeding of the 5000 (9:10–17)

Once again, it is believed that the disciples were the source of this miracle. It is surprising that no crowd reaction is given.

Luke seems to have made a mistake in recording this miracle. He sets the event in the town of Bethsaida, yet this does not make sense in view of the comment later on when the twelve Apostles ask Jesus to send the people away to the neighbouring towns and villages to buy food for we are in a lonely place here (9:12).

Some people have tried to explain away this miracle and suggested that the crowd merely shared what food they had with them. This sort of explanation misses completely the meaning of the story.

Why the Story was Remembered
The early Church, noting that this miracle took place in the wilderness, that is 'a lonely place', would have seen a parallel with the feeding of the children of Israel with manna in the wilderness of the Sinai desert. Just as God fed his children in the desert so now Jesus feeds his people in the lonely place.

Also, to early Christians, the story may have been seen as an anticipation of the Last Supper. Jesus blessed and broke the bread (9:16). Certainly this is how St John interpreted the story in his Gospel some forty years later (John 6).

Luke's Use of the Story
As well as interpreting the story as indicated above, Luke may have been showing Jesus as the Messiah. The Jews believed the reign of the Messiah would begin with a banquet. In this miracle there is a picture of the Messiah feeding his people. Such a picture points to the great Messianic feast in the future. The Messiah offers salvation; a way into that banquet.

SUMMARY

1   The miracle accounts are not historical reports of what happened. They are 'summaries' of the type of thing Jesus used to do.
2   Most of the miracles follow a set literary pattern.
3   The miracle accounts have been developed both by the early Church and Luke to say something important about Jesus.
4   The early Church used miracles to teach who they believed Jesus was; THE MESSIAH.
5   Luke also uses the miracles to say who Jesus is but the way he arranges his accounts shows that he is also interested in the AUTHORITY of Jesus; the SALVATION offered by Jesus and Jesus' conquest of evil.

6   Luke also uses the miracles to forward his view on universalism. The offer of Jesus is made to the sick, the poor and the bereaved of every nation, not just the Jews.

Study Skills

Knowledge

1   Name a miracle that shows 'active faith'.
2   Name a miracle that shows 'praying faith'.
3   What did the leper say to Jesus?
4   What did Jesus say to the paralysed man that angered the scribes?
5   In which miracle does Jesus touch the person he heals?
6   In which miracle does Jesus not meet either the person he heals or the person who requests the healing?
7   In which miracle is Jesus called 'son of David'?
8   How did Jesus calm the storm?
9   Where was Jesus when he raised the widow's son from the dead?
10   To whom did Jesus say, 'Your faith has cured you'?
12   Name one miracle that took place on the Sabbath.
13   Who did Jesus call a 'daughter of Abraham'?
14   Where was Jesus when he cured the man with dropsy?
15   Who returned to Jesus to thank him after he had been healed?

Understanding

16   Luke records three miracles of healing on the Sabbath. What do you understand to be the reasons why Jesus is criticised for healing on the Sabbath? Use illustrations from Luke's Gospel in your answer.
17   What do you understand to be the importance and place of faith in the healing miracles as recorded by Luke?

Evaluation

15   'The miracles were recorded because they comment on the person and work of Jesus'. Do you think this is true? Give examples in your answer.
16   Do you think that the nature miracles have any value in preaching the Christian message today? Give reasons for your answer.

Examination Practice

Describe briefly an incident when Jesus was criticised for healing a person. What had Jesus said or done that led to the criticism?   (4)

Choose *one* incident where Jesus shows his power over evil forces.
Describe the incident in your own words.   (4)
Using any miracle, illustrate the relationship between faith and
miracle.   (4)
Some people believe that the miracles, as recorded in the Gospel
did not happen. What are your views? Give reasons for your
answer.   (8)

Practical Work

● Produce a chart of the miracles in Luke. Make sure that the
  chart shows:

  (a) the exorcisms
  (b) the healing miracles commenting on Sabbath law
  (c) the healing miracles commenting on faith
  (d) the raising from the dead miracles
  (e) the nature miracles.

Also record on the chart any 'pronouncements' (see Chapter 1)
which Jesus makes in the miracles.

6 Discipleship

The purpose of this chapter is to examine the meaning, cost and reward of discipleship. This can be done by examining the following stories of discipleship.

– Stories of discipleship

1 The call of the first disciples (5:1–11; 5:27–28)
2 The appointment of the twelve apostles (6:12–16)
3 The sermon on the plain (6:20–49)
4 The mission of the twelve and of the seventy-two (9:1–6; 10:1–24)
5 The cost of discipleship (9:23–27; 9:57–62; 14:25–35)
6 How to pray (11:1–4)
7 Giving up possessions (18:18–30; 12:32–34; 16:13)
8 Who is the greatest? (22:24–27; 9:46–48)

Stories of Discipleship

The Call of the First Disciples (5:1–11; 5:27–28)

In Mark's Gospel the call of Peter, Andrew, James and John is a simple story where they respond to the command of Jesus: 'Follow me!'

In Luke the same purpose is achieved by the use of a miraculous occurrence. Jesus asked Simon if he may use his boat so that he could teach the large crowd that had come to the shore of the lake to hear him. When he had finished teaching he told Simon to pull out further into the lake and cast his nets over the side. Peter told Jesus that they had been fishing all night and had caught nothing. Nevertheless Peter did as he was told and found that the nets were full of fish to breaking point. Their friends in the other boat came to their aid. Simon, realising that Jesus was someone special, fell at his feet and said,

Go, Lord, leave me, sinner that I am! (5:8).

Jesus told them not to be afraid and said,

from now on you will be catching men (5:10).

At this Peter, James and John left their boats and followed him.

There are one or two problems with this story.

- Jesus commandeered Simon's boat. This is unusual if the two were complete strangers, as they were at this time.
- Simon feels 'sinful'. This can only be explained as a feeling of unworthiness in the presence of one who had just performed the miracle.
- Simon calls Jesus 'Lord'. This is impossible at this time as this title was not used of Jesus until after the resurrection.
- In most Greek manuscripts Simon is referred to in this story as Simon Peter. The name Peter is a nickname meaning 'rock' and was not given to Simon until later.

One explanation that answers all the difficulties is that Luke is using a story out of context. In John's Gospel there is a similar story which takes place after the resurrection (John 21:1–19). If the original setting of the story is after the resurrection, and Luke has changed its historical setting, then the problems are removed.

By the time of the post-resurrection period:

- Jesus and Simon were extremely well known to each other.
- Simon had become Peter the rock.
- Simon would call Jesus Lord.
- Jesus could occupy Simon's boat at will.
- Simon had a deep sense of sin because of his denial of Jesus at the time of the arrest.

At the time Luke was writing,the sign of the fish had become a symbol, for early Christians, of Jesus' presence with them in their work of preaching the Gospel. The instruction to Simon and his friends to 'catch men' would be seen as an instruction to all Christians.

THE FISH

The Greek word for fish is 'Ichthus'. The early Christians used this word as a secret sign of their faith. If the Greek letters making up the word are taken separately then they stand for an early confession of faith.

```
I    = Jesus      = Jesus
CH  = Christos    = Christ
```

TH = Theou   = of God
U   = unios   = Son
S   = soter   = Saviour

JESUS CHRIST, SON OF GOD, SAVIOUR

The other disciple called by Jesus was a tax collector called Levi who was at work in the customs house. Jesus told him to follow and Levi

> rose to his feet, left everything behind, and followed him (5:28).

The tax collectors were extremely unpopular people with the Jews because they were, in the main, Jews who acted for the Romans. This was frowned upon by most Jews. The situation was made worse by the cheating that went on. The tax collectors were allowed to collect more than was necessary and pocket the difference (19:1–10). Most people detested the tax collectors and Jesus himself was severely criticised for his association with them.

Discipleship today

This calling of disciples still happens today. This is what the word 'vocation' means. People who have a vocation to the priesthood, ordained ministry or religious orders, are required to turn their backs on personal wishes and commit themselves to God regardless of cost. For some, as in the Roman Catholic Church, this means taking a vow of celibacy; for some entering religious orders it means taking the vows of celibacy, poverty and obedience.

The question of vocation, however, can be more widely applied to the whole question of being a Christian. The Christian considers discipleship to be a vocation. Vocation, therefore, is expressed through the different aspects of life, for example, through marriage, work and relationships with others.

The Appointment of the Twelve Apostles (6:12–16)

After Jesus had been criticised for curing the man with the withered arm and the Pharisees and lawyers were, in their anger, discussing what they could do about it, Jesus went into the hills to pray. The next morning he appointed twelve special men from among the larger group of disciples. These twelve Jesus called Apostles (appointed ones). From that time the apostles were distinguished from the general company of Jesus' disciples.

THE APOSTLES NAMED BY LUKE (6:14–16)

1 Simon:	given the nickname 'Peter'.
2 Andrew:	Simon's brother.
3 James	
4 John	
5 Philip	
6 Bartholomew	
7 Matthew:	This was probably Levi. Matthew's Gospel names him as Matthew the tax-collector.
8 Thomas	
9 James:	the son of Alphaeus.
10 Simon:	the Zealot; that is, a nationalist or revolutionary who wished to fight against the Romans.
11 Judas:	the son of James.
12 Judas Iscariot:	The name Iscariot may mean 'man from Kerioth' or it could be from the Latin word 'sicarius' which means 'assassin' or 'Zealot'.

The twelve Apostles stand for the twelve tribes of Israel as opposed to those who might be expected to represent Israel such as the Jewish leaders. These are the men who are now to be found in the company of Jesus and to whom he gives the Apostolic appointment.

Discipleship today

Some Christian Churches, notably the Roman Catholic Church, consider that the Apostles represent today in the persons of their successors, the bishops of the Church. They would also claim that the Pope is the successor to St Peter, regarded as the first Pope. The Church of England would also claim this unbroken succession. Other Christian denominations such as the Methodist Church make no such claims regarding their ministers.

Once again, on a wider basis, the task of the Christian Church in discipleship is the same as it was at the time of Jesus. Christians believe the Church is the body of Christ and as such all share in its Apostolic mission.

The Sermon on the Plain (6:20–49)

The Sermon on the Plain, reported by Luke, is given to the disciples and therefore, must be meant to apply to Christian discipleship. The Sermon is a collection of different teachings and was probably not delivered at the same time. An analysis of the passage is helpful to see the different themes that are contained in the Sermon.

Beatitudes and Woes (6:20–26)
The word 'beatitude' means 'blessed'. Some translations use the word 'happy'. It is a term of encouragement. Luke mentions four such encouragements.

How blest are those in need, the hungry, those who weep and those who are persecuted because of Jesus. Their reward will be a rich one in the kingdom of heaven.

In contrast, alas for those who are now rich, well-fed, happy and have a position of flattery among men. Their reward is found in those things alone.

Jesus is not condemning these kind of people but pointing out that they are self-satisfied. Such an attitude is not one for a disciple to adopt.

Love of Enemies (6:27–36)
Jesus told his disciples that they must love their enemies, and went on to say what Christian love is. It is an active doing of good, even to those who are enemies; an attitude of blessing not cursing, coupled with prayer for their wellbeing. The examples Jesus gives of how this love shows itself in action (6:29–31) reach a climax with the stating of the simplest code, governing all Christian behaviour; the golden rule,

> Treat others as you would like them to treat you (6:31).

It is easy to love and do good to those who behave in like manner but the disciple must go further and extend the same attitude to the enemy. He must copy God who is compassionate and who

is kind to the ungrateful and wicked (6:35).

Do Not Judge (6:37–42)
It is not the role of the disciples to indulge in harsh judgment or criticism of others. Rather they are to 'acquit' and 'give' and in so doing receive an overwhelming amount of gifts from God in return (6:37–38).

Jesus then goes on to give two examples.

1 The blind cannot lead the blind. In other words, the disciples must see clearly before they can hope to guide others.
2 Jesus then gave a proverb full of humour. A person with a plank in his eye is hardly in a position to remove a speck from another person's eye. The meaning of this is that a person with many faults cannot help another to be rid of one small fault.

The Result of Discipleship (6:43–45)
Using the illustration of a good and bad tree producing opposite fruits, Jesus is teaching that only good can produce good and bad produce bad. The disciple must make sure that his own heart is right.

The Parable of the Housebuilders (6:46–49)
The Sermon concludes with the parable of the two housebuilders, one of whom built his house on rock and the other, on soil. The first withstands the ravages of the storm, the second is washed away. The disciple, if he listens to the words of Jesus and acts on them, builds his life on rock.

Discipleship today

The Sermon on the Plain still has relevance for the Christian disciples of today. It teaches what the Christian attitude should be towards other people.
- *This attitude should have, at all times, a concern for the poor, hungry and sorrowful.*
- *It should be prepared to be rejected and even hated.*
- *It should take no pride in self-sufficiency. It must be an attitude founded in the love of God.*
- *The Christian must love the enemy with a practical goodness.*

- *The golden rule is still to treat other people as you would wish to be treated.*
- *It is not the role of the disciple to act as judge. He must not condemn others.*
- *The disciple must pay particular attention to his own standards of faith and behaviour and not attempt to correct others' faults which may not be as great as his own.*
- *It is the duty of the disciple to hear the words of Jesus and act on them.*

Some people would say that the Church falls far short of these standards as it seems to set itself up as a superior group, and even judges those who do not wish to belong to it.

Indeed, there are times when this seems to be so. The Church must always be aware that it has no overriding position of authority in the affairs of people other than in the affairs of those who have committed themselves to it. It is not the role of the people of the Church to judge, condemn or be superior. Their task is to care for all those in need; to love in a completely self-denying way of goodness, and to be faithful to the words of Christ.

The Mission of the Twelve and of the Seventy-Two (9:1–6; 10:1–24)

Luke records two missions, the first by the twelve Apostles and the second by seventy-two disciples. Both groups were to conduct their mission under strict conditions.

The Twelve	The Seventy-Two
	They were to go out in pairs
Take nothing for the journey	
No staff	
No haversack	No haversack
No bread	
No money	No money
	Travel barefoot
No second coat	

	Exchange no greeting on the road
Stay in one place	Stay in one place
	'Peace to this house'
	Eat the food provided for you
Shake the dust from the feet if you are not made welcome	Shake the dust from your feet if not made welcome

Both groups were given tasks:

The Twelve	The Seventy-two
They were to overcome devils	
They were to cure diseases and heal	Heal the sick
They were to proclaim the kingdom of God	Say 'the kingdom of God has come close to you'

Both groups of missionaries were to go in a spirit of self denial, travelling light. They were obviously intended to make short journeys from village to village. They were to depend on hospitality for their daily needs and to accept it gratefully. 'Shaking the dust from the feet' was a Jewish custom when coming back into their own country from Gentile territory. Jesus extends this symbolism to anyone who will not welcome the disciples, both Jew and Gentile. They were not to waste their time on those who did not respond. Their ministry was one of healing of the body, mind and spirit.

ADDITIONAL NOTE ON THE MISSION OF THE SEVENTY-TWO

- Some early manuscripts state that there were seventy not seventy-two disciples.
- Both numbers are symbolic. Seventy represents the seventy leaders chosen by Moses to help him lead the children of Israel in the journey through the Sinai desert after their escape from Egypt.

Seventy-two represents the number, according to the Jews, of all the nations of the world. It may be that Luke is pointing to one of his major themes, that of universalism. The passage is symbolic of the world-wide mission of the Church.

- Various towns are mentioned in the passage. Sodom was the wicked city condemned in the Old Testament. Chorazin, Tyre and Sidon were regarded as being wicked cities of the Gentile world. Capernaum and Bethsaida are two places that rejected Jesus.

- When the seventy-two return to Jesus, they are full of joy. Jesus welcomes them with the words,

  I have given you the power to tread underfoot snakes and scorpions and all the forces of the enemy (10:19).

  This should not be taken literally. The meaning is symbolic, the snakes and scorpions standing for evil.

- The story of the mission of the seventy-two closes with a prayer of Jesus (10:21–22). This prayer is very similar to those found in John's Gospel, where John describes a close relationship between Jesus and his Father. The prayer reflects the closest relationship between Jesus and God to be found in Luke's Gospel.

Discipleship today

In essence the mission of the Church today remains the same. Modern day disciples still go out to preach the kingdom of God. The missionary scene may well have changed in the twentieth century but the principle remains the same. All Christian churches still work throughout the world:

- *caring for the sick;*
- *feeding the hungry;*
- *fighting against evil injustice in many countries;*
- *preaching the message of the kingdom of God through medical, educational, social, agricultural and even political ways.*

Christian organisations, such as Christian Aid, Cafod, and many others, carry on, in modern ways using modern methods, the missions of the Apostles and disciples of Jesus.

The Cost of Discipleship (9:23–27; 9:57–62; 14:25–35)

Jesus gives a clear indication of the cost of discipleship just after the profession of faith by Peter and the first prediction of the suffering, death and resurrection of Jesus (9:18–22).

> If anyone wishes to be a follower of mine, he must leave self behind; day after day he must take up his cross, and come with me (9:23).

In this passage is found the hardest saying of Jesus about discipleship. It is important to understand what Jesus meant by these words.

(a) **To leave self behind**. This does not just mean to deny oneself. It does not mean going without pleasures as so many people do, for example, in the period of Lent. To leave self behind means to put oneself last in all things; to have no care about one's own life and to desire no rights or privileges except that of belonging to God.

(b) **To take up the cross day after day**. Luke has added the words 'day after day' and in so doing weakens the original saying found in Mark because it is impossible to take up the cross more than once. Luke means by the words the bearing of hardship and burdens for the sake of the faith. Most people today interpret the words in the Lukan way. 'We all have our cross to bear' has become a modern day expression meaning a burden or anxiety.

Originally, Jesus meant something much more frightening. For many Christians of the first century and every century since, their fate was to take up the cross literally and die for their faith in Christ. Discipleship means being prepared to follow Jesus to the point of death.

(c) **Come with me**. This command only makes sense when put in the context of the teaching that comes immediately before it. Jesus has just stated that he is going to suffer and die. The invitation to go with him is an invitation to follow along the same path. Discipleship can involve suffering and death.

On the one hand to those who do respond there will be the reward of safety. On the other hand if a disciple seeks to receive, he will in the end lose everything (9:24–25). If the disciple is ashamed of belonging to Christ, then he must not be surprised if Christ is ashamed of him (9:26).

The passage ends with a difficult saying:

> there are some of those standing here who will not taste death before they have seen the kingdom of God (9:27).

It is not clear to what Jesus is referring. There are three possible alternatives:

1 the second coming of Christ mentioned in the previous verse (this is called the Parousia). The only difficulty with this view is that Jesus made a mistake because the Parousia has not yet happened and those 'standing there' are long since dead;
2 the Transfiguration, a story that comes immediately after this saying on discipleship;
3 the birth of the Christian Church at Pentecost.

It is perhaps much more likely that the sentence refers to another occasion altogether and that the original setting of the saying has been lost.

In the second passage dealing with the cost of discipleship (9:57–62) Jesus again stresses that discipleship is a matter of both urgency and total commitment. The passage deals with the answers Jesus gave to three people who asked about discipleship.

(a) The first offered to follow unreservedly.

> 'I will follow you wherever you go' (9:57).

The comment of Jesus is one of warning. Even foxes and birds have their resting places but the disciple cannot count on even that security.

(b) The second made an excuse to the command 'follow me'.

> Let me go and bury my father first (9:59).

Jesus' reply may seem a little harsh but it must be seen in context. Jesus is not saying that the man should not bury his father for this duty had to be done. It does not follow that the man's father was in fact dead, only that he could not become a disciple until his father had died. It was an excuse and discipleship is not founded on excuses.

(c) The third is willing to follow but makes an excuse.

> I will follow you, sir, but let me first say good-bye
> to my people at home (9:61).

The inference is that the man has doubts. He is unsure of his willingness to follow. Jesus answered that a would-be disciple cannot hesitate, or look back. He must be committed.

Through these three examples it can be seen that there can be no room for hesitation, excuse or even bravado in the matter of discipleship.

The third passage (14–25–35) contains some strong words on the cost of discipleship. A careful interpretation is necessary.

> If anyone comes to me and does not hate his father
> and mother, wife and children, brothers and sisters,
> even his own life, he cannot be a disciple of mine
> (14:26).

Jesus is not saying that his disciples must HATE their families. The word 'hate' in Hebrew means to give second place, not to detest; to love one more than the other. The disciple must put Jesus first. The cost of doing this is great and Jesus goes on to give two little parables about counting the cost.

1   The man who is building a tower is wise only if he estimates the cost first to see if he can afford it.
2   The king who is going to war is wise only if he works out that his army is strong enough. Otherwise it would be best to pursue peace.

It is the same with discipleship. It is necessary to calculate the cost of becoming a disciple.

The final remarks in this passage about the salt (14:34–35) describe worthless disciples. Salt was used for preserving and seasoning food. If salt were to lose its taste it would be useless. So disciples who have lost their 'taste', that is, their desire to follow Jesus, are also useless.

Discipleship today

Discipleship still involves suffering and death for many Christians in the world today. In the twentieth century, many Christians have suffered martyrdom for their faith. Hundreds of clergy and laity, both Roman Catholic and Protestant, lost their lives in the Germany of the Third Reich. Many hundreds have been killed in the political struggles of South America, in the missionary work of the Church in Africa and in the fight for religious freedom in many countries behind the Iron Curtain.

The twentieth century has its own Christian martyrs: St Maximilian Kolbe, Dietrich Bonhoeffer, Archbishop Romero, to name but three. For each one remembered there are many more whose names are little remembered but who suffered death because they were disciples of Christ.

How to Pray (11:1–4)

On one occasion, after Jesus had finished praying, his disciples asked him to teach them to pray. In reply Jesus instructed them in what has become known as the 'Our Father' or 'Lord's Prayer'.

This prayer, which, in Luke's version, is generally believed to be closest to the words spoken by Jesus, is a masterpiece of summary of the teaching of Jesus.

> Father, thy name be hallowed;

In this very simple sentence Jesus taught his disciples to revere the fatherhood of God.

> thy kingdom come.

Jesus taught them to pray that the rule of God would be set up on earth.

> Give us each day our daily bread.

The Greek phrase used at this point really means 'give us today our bread for tomorrow'. Jesus taught his disciples to ask God simply for the basic necessities of life. Bread stands for more than just food.

> and forgive us our sins,
> for we too forgive all who have done us wrong.

The disciples are taught the important truth that God's forgiveness is related to their forgiveness of each other.

> And do not bring us to the test.

The disciples are to ask for God's protection each day in all that they do.

Discipleship today

- *Many Christians today would claim that the image of God as Father or parent is the warmest and most personal of all the symbols used of God and he must be treated with a deep and holy respect.*
- *They continue to pray and work for the coming of God's kingdom for that is what the calling to be a disciple means.*
- *They see God as the provider of the necessities of life and try to put their trust in him.*
- *They consider that forgiveness and reconciliation are fundamental to the Christian faith.*
- *They believe it is important to ask God to prevent them from being placed in situations of temptation. It is important to note that most Christians do not believe that God himself puts people to the test in the sense of trying to trap them. This view would be incompatible with the belief in a God of love.*

Giving Up Possessions (18:18–30; 12:32–34; 16:13)

The first passage is about a man of the ruling class who went to Jesus and asked the question,

> what must I do to win eternal life? (*18:18*).

Jesus reminded him of the Commandments and the man replied that he had been obedient since childhood. Jesus then went on to say that there was still one thing that prevented him from being a disciple. He must give up his wealth and give it to the poor. The demand was too great. The man's heart sank.

It is important to realise that Jesus is not teaching that each person who becomes a disciple must give up all he or she possesses. What he is saying is that discipleship is a matter of commitment and this involves demands. The demand may vary according to the particular person. Simon Peter had to give up his livelihood on the fishing boats, Levi, his job as a tax collector. For some people it has been the giving up of family, parents or friends. For others it has meant the giving up of the security of a home in order to serve Jesus in foreign countries as missionaries, priests or teachers. The sacrifices are endless.

It must be realised, however, that the possession of riches presents a special problem. Jesus went on to say,

> How hard it is for the wealthy to enter the kingdom
> of God (18:24).

He gave a most peculiar illustration.

> It is easier for a camel to go through the eye of a
> needle than for a rich man to enter the kingdom of
> God (18:25).

This is a difficult saying. Some scholars have suggested that
the original word was 'rope' not 'camel', as the words in
Greek are very similar. Others have suggested that one of the
small gates in Jerusalem was called the 'Needle Eye', through
which a camel could only pass with some difficulty. Whatever
the interpretation, Jesus is teaching that wealth can be a
barrier to discipleship.

The second passage contains further advice to the disciples
on the subject of discipleship and wealth. Jesus told them,

> Sell your possessions and give in charity . . . for
> where your treasure is, there will your heart be also
> (12:33–34).

A person's commitment is a matter of the heart. It cannot be
in competition with the desire for wealth.

The third passage is a well known single verse on the
subject of money.

> No servant can be the slave of two masters; for
> either he will hate the first and love the second, or
> he will be devoted to the first and think nothing of
> the second. You cannot serve God and Money
> (16:13).

Jesus is saying that money can usurp the place of God.

Discipleship today

*The danger with wealth is that it can separate a person from
God. The reason for this is that if a person becomes obsessed with
riches then he has little time for God. Money takes the place of
God (16:13). Again it must be stated that this same teaching
applies to many other things besides wealth and possessions.*

*The main teaching of these stories is that discipleship involves
a commitment that involves and demands sacrifice.*

*The story ends with Peter claiming that all of them have given
up their belongings in order to follow Jesus (18:28). In return
Jesus promised:*

> there is no one who has given up home, or wife,
> brothers, parents, or children, for the sake of the
> kingdom of God, who will not be repaid many times
> over in this age, and in the age to come have eternal
> life (18:29–30).

What this means is that discipleship does not mean poverty. It means real life here and now and life with God in eternity. One way, for example, that this promise can be fulfilled is in the fellowship of the Church, which is the family of God.

Who is the Greatest? (22:24–27; 9:46–48)

Luke has two stories about the disciples arguing amongst themselves as to who was the greatest. They are obviously from the same root.

This main story happens at the Last Supper. Even though Jesus has just announced that someone is going to betray him, the thought of the Apostles is which of them is to be regarded as the greatest. Once again Jesus began to teach them the true nature of discipleship. Discipleship should not involve quarrelling about greatness. He taught them the difference between greatness and humility. The only way to greatness was to serve others.

> The highest among you must bear himself like the
> youngest, the chief of you like a servant (22:26).

He gives the example of the relationship between a person sitting at the table and the one who serves the meal. In those times the person sitting at the table was considered superior to the servant. Jesus says that as far as his disciples are concerned this is not so. He points to himself as the supreme example. He has come as the servant (22:27). The disciple must imitate the example of the master.

In the second story Jesus uses the example of a little child for the disciples to follow. The child is the weakest member of the community. To receive the weak and the humble, that is, a little child, is to receive not only Jesus himself but also God.

Discipleship today

This is still the calling of the Christian disciple. Sometimes the opposite seems to be the case. Some people point out that most established Churches have a structure that seems to be a ranking of greatness and position. In the Episcopal Churches there are the Holy Orders of Bishop, Priest and Deacon. Amongst these are other less familiar titles which seem to support the idea of rank, such as Cardinal, Archbishop, Canon, Dean and Vicar. In the non-conformist tradition, the titles are less universal but still seem to indicate rank; Moderator, President, Chairman and Superintendent. Finally there are the laity, some of whom also have titles such as Church Warden, Steward and Elder.

It should be remembered that all these positions are not positions of greatness. They are positions of service. Some are called to the privilege of Holy Orders or Ministry in order that they may, in humility, be servants of the Church. If this is not clearly visible, then it is the weakness of the men and women in these positions and not the positions themselves that are at fault. To serve in humility is the foundation of Christian discipleship for all and every single individual in the Christian Church.

SUMMARY

- The word 'disciple' means a 'follower'.
- Some people are called to leave everything and follow Jesus regardless of cost. This calling is known as a 'vocation'.
- All disciples must have a wholehearted commitment to Jesus.
- A disciple is one who puts himself last in all things.
- Discipleship means being prepared to follow Jesus even if it means suffering, rejection and death.
- The nature of discipleship is not one of privilege, position or greatness but is one of humble service.
- A disciple is one who has a concern for other people and their problems.
- A disciple must not be arrogant but tolerant and receptive to the views of others.
- A disciple must be aware of the danger of such obsessions as wealth and be single-minded in discipleship.

Study Skills

Knowledge

1 Give a short account of the call of the first disciples as recorded by Luke.
2 What was the occupation of Levi?
3 Name the two sets of brothers in the list of the twelve Apostles as recorded by Luke.
4 What should the attitude of disciples be towards enemies?
5 Give an account of the Parable of the Housebuilders with which Luke concludes the Sermon on the Plain.
6 What were the twelve Apostles sent out to do on their mission?
7 What excuses did some people make when challenged to become disciples?
8 What did the man need to do, who asked Jesus 'Good master, what must I do to win eternal life?'
9 Complete the quotation: 'You cannot serve God and . . .'
10 How does Jesus use a child as an example of discipleship?

Understanding

11 Jesus said the disciple must 'leave self behind; day after day he must take up his cross, and come with me'. What do you understand Jesus to mean by these words?
12 What do you understand to be the qualities of discipleship found in the Sermon on the Plain?

Evaluation

13 Do you think it is possible to be a disciple today in the way Jesus intended? What are the dangers facing the disciple in the modern world?
14 Do you think it is true to say that all Christians have a vocation? If so, in what ways can vocation be expressed today?

Examination Practice

What were the instructions Jesus gave when he sent out the seventy-two disciples? (5)
What is the significance of the number seventy-two? (3)
Explain the meaning of the words 'the very dust of your town that clings to your feet we wipe off to your shame'. (4)
On which other occasion did Jesus send out disciples on a mission? (1)
'The mission of the seventy-two cannot be applied to the twentieth century'. Do you agree with this statement? Give reasons for your answer. (7)

Practical Work

Research and prepare a paragraph on one or more of the following Christians who lost their lives because they were followers of Jesus:
– Rev Dr Martin Luther King
– Archbishop Romero
– St Maximilian Kolbe
– Dietrich Bonhoeffer

7 The Suffering and Death of Jesus

The suffering and death of Jesus is an important part of Luke's Gospel. Considerable time must be given to its study. There are three areas of study to be covered.
- The narrative of the Jerusalem ministry and the Passion.
- The Jerusalem Ministry
- To answer the question, 'Why did Jesus have to die?'
- What does the death of Jesus mean for Christians today?

The Narrative of the Jerusalem Ministry and the Passion

Unlike Mark, Luke does not arrange the events of the last days of Jesus into a one week period. He tries to give the impression that the events in Jerusalem, leading up to the crucifixion, cover a longer period of time (see 19:47; 20:1; 21:38; 22:1; 22:7). In spite of this the narrative in Luke covers the same basic events found in Mark.

The events of the Jerusalem ministry can be tabled. It must be remembered that the Jewish day begins at 6.00 pm.

THE JERUSALEM MINISTRY
ONE DAY

The entry into Jerusalem 19:28–40
The lament for Jerusalem 19:41–44
The expulsion of the traders from the Temple 19:45–48

ANOTHER TIME

The question of authority 20:1–8
The Parable of the Tenants 20:9–19
The question of paying taxes to Caesar 20:20–26
The question about resurrection 20:27–44
Criticism of the Scribes 20:45–47
The widow's mite 21:1–4
Discourse on the destruction of Jerusalem and the end of the world 21:5–38

The Jerusalem Ministry

One day

The Entry into Jerusalem (19:28–40)
The claim of Jesus to be the Messiah was made public as he rode a donkey down 'the descent from the mount of Olives' towards the city. This action emphasised the fact that he was a peaceful Messiah and not the military leader who would drive out the Romans, which was the popular idea of the Messiah at that time.

Luke does not have the people spreading palm branches but they spread their coats and joyfully praise God. He quotes Psalm 118:25–26:

> Blessings on him who comes as king in the name of the Lord! *(19:38),*

so informing his readers that the people recognised Jesus as Messiah. The words of the Psalm, however, were used also to call down a blessing on pilgrims entering the city for the festival of Passover. It is not clear, therefore, if the ordinary people would have seen any real meaning in the action of Jesus.

Nevertheless Luke emphasises the Messiahship of Jesus by adding to the quotation from the Psalm, the words,

> Peace in heaven, glory in highest heaven! (*19:38*).

These words are very similar to those found in the song of the 'heavenly host' at the birth of Jesus, when the angel of the Lord pronounces the Messiahship of Jesus to the shepherds (2:11–14). Christians celebrate, each year, Jesus' triumphant ride as Messiah, on Palm Sunday, the Sunday before Easter day.

The Lament for Jerusalem (19:41–44)
When Jesus approached the city he

> wept over it (*19:41*).

Luke indicates that Jesus knew that Jerusalem was soon to be destroyed. This was to happen in 70 AD.

Some scholars think that Luke is writing with hindsight at this point, as he describes the siege of Jerusalem and the events that followed in detail. The reason given for the impending destruction of the city is that the people, in spite of their warm welcome of Jesus as he rode into the city as Messiah, do not really understand. In a very short time these same people will be calling for Jesus to be put to death.

The Expulsion of the Traders from the Temple (19:45–48)
In the prophecy of Malachi it says, 'Suddenly the Lord whom you seek will come to his Temple' (Malachi 3:1). It may be that this prophecy lies behind the account of the expulsion of the traders from the Temple. These traders sold sacrifices to pilgrims coming to Jerusalem. Such sacrifices had to be bought with special Temple money because foreign currency showed the heads of pagan rulers or gods, and such objects were forbidden in the Temple by the Law.

Jesus, in challenging the use of the Temple for such trading, also challenged the authority of the chief priests, who allowed it to take place. The words of Jesus are a combination of Isaiah 56:7 and Jeremiah 7:11: 'my house shall be called a house of prayer for all the nations but you have made it into a robbers' cave' (19:46).

It is surprising that Jesus could get away with such a challenge to the authority of the priests. Luke records that as Jesus taught in the Temple day by day, the chief priests and the lawyers looked for some way of getting rid of him but could not because he was, at that time, popular with the people.

They

'hung upon his words' (*19:48*).

Another Time

The question of authority (20:1–8) (see chapter 3)
The Parable of the Tenants (20:9–19) (see chapter 4)
The question of paying taxes to Caesar (20:20–26) (see chapter 3)
The question about resurrection (20:27–44) (see chapter 3)
Criticism of the Scribes (20:45–47) (see chapter 3)

The Widow's Mite (21:1–4)
The temple treasury was located in the Court of Women in the Temple. There were chests into which people could place their offerings. Jesus drew the sharp contrast between the widow who gave everything she had, and the rich people who were merely giving from their surplus, even though they gave more than the widow.

Discourse on the Destruction of Jerusalem and the End of the World (21:5–38)
The main problem with this section of Luke's account is that it seems to be dealing with two distinct themes:

1   the fall of Jerusalem in AD 70
2   the second coming of the Son of Man

Some scholars have suggested that these verses, obviously based on the apocalyptic chapter in Mark's Gospel, are a combination of two different sources. They contain the teaching of Jesus about the coming destruction of the capital city. Into this has been inserted other Christian apocalyptic material about the end of the world.

WHAT IS APOCALYPTIC WRITING?

● The Greek word 'apocalypse' means 'unveiling' or 'revealing' a secret.

- The word 'apocalyptic' was used for writings that spoke about the future in the sense of events that only God could know and was prepared to 'reveal'.
- Apocalyptic writing often used highly symbolic picture language.
- This kind of writing has its origin in Jewish history. The Jews believed that God controlled everything and that at the end of time he would establish his rule over the whole world. The idea of God setting up his final rule over all things is called 'eschatology'. This word literally means 'at the end'.
- In the second century BC, the Jews were conquered by the Greeks. The belief that God would still bring about his final rule over the whole of the human race took on a new significance. The ideas about the end of the world began to be written in terms of catastrophe. The wicked would come to a violent end and God would rule supreme surrounded by the good. This type of writing was called 'apocalyptic'.
- The language of apocalyptic writing is very vivid. It is full of supernatural wonder, angels and visions of good and evil.
- Apocalyptic writing normally arose at times of great suffering and persecution. Its aim is to encourage the faithful. The best example of apocalyptic writing in the Old Testament is the book of Daniel. In the New Testament the major example is the Book of Revelation.

The analysis of this section is as follows:
21:5–7
The discourse is introduced by the reporting of a conversation between Jesus and his disciples about the Temple. Some people were commenting on the magnificence of the Temple when Jesus announced that there would come a time when it would be destroyed. The Temple was begun in the reign of Herod the Great in 20 BC. At the time of Jesus it was unfinished (see Chapter 1).

Jesus, aware that the Jews' relationships with their Roman masters would finally end in disaster, forecast that the Temple would be destroyed. This was to happen in AD 70, six years after it was completed.

The disciples ask him when this will happen. The question does not seem to receive a direct answer. Luke uses it as an introduction to a more general teaching about the end of the world as well as the destruction of Jerusalem.

Jesus' answer to the question is given later on in the discourse.

21:8–9; 12–19

These verses contain warnings given to the disciples. They are probably based on words said by Jesus on different occasions but have been gathered together to teach about the dangers of being a disciple.

The teaching of the verses is clear:

1   Disciples must beware of those who falsely claim to be the Christ (21:8)
2   They must be on their guard for they would undergo persecution, arrest, appearances in court and imprisonment. They must not be over-awed by such experiences for Jesus himself would give them the ability to speak with a wisdom that would be able to meet opposition and resistance.
3   They must also be on their guard against betrayal. Families will be split. To be a Christian may bring hatred and even death.

21:10–11

This is typical apocalyptic language with its emphasis on war, earthquakes, famines and plagues. These are the signs that will precede the end of the world.

21:20–24

The original questions about the Temple now receive answers.

> What will be the sign when it is due to happen? (*21:7*)

Jerusalem would be placed under siege and destroyed by the Romans. The warnings given reflect the idea of approaching armies and fleeing before them. It must be remembered that Luke is writing after the event and is therefore able to be more precise in his account than Mark was, who was writing before the event.

> When will it all come about? (*21:7*).

The only answer to the timing of the event of destruction is found later in the chapter, when he says,

> I tell you this: the present generation will live to see it all (21:32).

21:25–28
This passage is couched in typical apocalyptic language. The end is to be preceded by cosmic disorder. Then the Son of Man will come and liberation will be at hand. The verse regarding the 'Son of Man' is a quotation from the apocalyptic book of Daniel (Daniel 7:13–14), but Luke intends it to relate to Jesus' second coming.
21:29–31
Luke then relates the parable of the fig-tree. A tree breaking into leaf heralds the approach of summer. In the same way, all these signs herald the time when the kingdom of God draws near.
21:34–36
The discourse ends with the warning to be alert. Luke is saying that despite all the signs, the end will come suddenly. It is the task of the Christian to be alert and watchful.

What Christians believe about the Second Coming of Jesus

In the Old Testament the belief developed that the Son of Man would come to his own people and set up the rule of God on earth. This belief was carried forward into the Christian era.
Christians today interpret this in three main ways.

1   *Some Christians see the coming of Jesus, born in Bethlehem, as the coming of the Son of Man. They believe that in Jesus, God has visited his people and that in the life, death and resurrection of Jesus, the new era of God's kingdom has already been established.*
2   *Others believe that Jesus' resurrection is to be interpreted as his return in glory as the Son of Man.*
3   *Still others believe, as the early Church did, that there will come a time in the future when Jesus will come again. At that time he will establish God's rule on earth for all to see. When this will happen no one knows but God himself.*

Study Skills

Knowledge

1 What instructions did Jesus give when he sent his disciples to fetch the colt?
2 What did the disciples sing aloud when Jesus rode the colt towards Jerusalem?
3 Why did Jesus weep when he came in sight of the city?
4 How did the Jewish leaders react to the cleansing of the Temple?
5 Which building were the disciples talking about when they commented on its 'fine stones'?
6 What does the word 'apocalypse' mean?
7 Name three things that Jesus says will happen to the disciples before the end.
8 Name the three heavenly 'signs' that will precede the coming of the Son of Man.

Understanding

9 What do you think is the meaning of the story of Jesus' riding the colt towards Jerusalem?
10 What do you understand to be the theme or themes of the apocalyptic discourse in Luke's Gospel? Give examples in your answer.

Evaluation

11 What do you think Luke means by the return of the Son of Man? How do you think Christians interpret the signs of the second coming in Luke's Gospel?

Sometime before Thursday

The Plot Against Jesus (22:1–2)
The story of the Passion continues with the statement that the chief priests and doctors of the Law were wondering how to do away with Jesus. They were afraid of the reaction of the people because Jesus was still popular with them.

Luke states that this happened just before the approaching feast of Unleavened Bread

'known as Passover' (22:1).

This is not strictly accurate as they were two distinct feasts.

FESTIVAL OF UNLEAVENED BREAD

- Originally, this was a separate feast to Passover.
- By the time of Jesus the two festivals were celebrated at the same time.
- Leaven was a substance used to make bread rise.
- It was a piece of dough kept back from the previous baking.
- The main symbol of the feast was the use of unleavened (flat) bread for a whole week.
- This was to symbolise a break with the past and all its sin and the making of a fresh start.

Judas Plans his Betrayal (22:3–6)
Luke states that the devil entered into Judas and as a result of this influence he went to the chief priests and officers of the Temple police to talk about betraying Jesus.

The first question to ask is 'why did Judas betray Jesus?'

Various suggestions have been made as to why Judas betrayed Jesus:

(a) Mark does not make it clear what the motive of Judas was in betraying Jesus.
(b) Matthew makes Judas out to be a greedy man who wanted money. The amount of money was not very large. Matthew claims it was thirty pieces of silver, which was the Old Testament price of a slave.
(c) John agrees with Luke that Judas was influenced by the devil. He goes further than Luke and not only calls Judas a thief but also says that he was chosen by God to perform the evil deed.
(d) It has been suggested that the real reason Judas betrayed Jesus was because he wanted Jesus to be the popular Messiah of the day who would drive out the Romans. He was disappointed that such a course of action seemed to be the last thing in Jesus' mind.

The second question is, 'What does the betrayal of Jesus really mean?' These are two views of which the first is the most popular.

1   The betrayal was the leading of the Temple police to Jesus. After all, before Jesus could be arrested he must be

found. Judas knew where he would be. The authorities needed someone to lead them to where Jesus was so that he could be arrested quietly.

2   The second reason suggested is that Judas told the chief priests that Jesus had claimed to be some sort of Messiah; perhaps one who would lead a rebellion against the Romans.

Thursday (6.00 pm Wed – 6.00 pm Thurs)

Preparations for the Passover (22:7–13)
The disciples are sent, by pre-arranged signal, to prepare a room in the city where the Passover could be celebrated that evening. Luke makes it clear that the preparations were for a Passover meal. There is considerable dispute, however, as to whether the Last Supper was a Passover meal. It has been argued that Jesus could not have been executed on the feast day of the Passover because:

1   The priests would not have held a trial on a feast day.
2   The execution on a feast day was impossible according to Jewish law.

Scholars holding this opinion point to other information to support their view:

- The food usually eaten at Passover such as the lamb and bitter herbs is not mentioned.
- There is no reference to the special story of the escape of the Jews from Egypt used at the Passover celebration (This story is called the Haggadah).
- John's Gospel claims that the Passover was held that year, on the Sabbath (6.00 pm Fri – 6.00 pm Sat). Jesus was, therefore, dead before the Passover day began. The meal he celebrated with his disciples cannot have been the Passover meal.

This problem can be answered quite easily. At the time of Jesus there was a dispute between the Pharisees and Sadducees as to when the festival of Passover began. The Pharisees were allowed to hold the meal one day before the official date. Jesus may have been following the custom of the Pharisees by celebrating the Passover on the Thursday evening. There is no doubt that Luke intends his readers to understand the Last Supper as the Passover meal.

Friday (6.00 pm Thurs – 6.00 pm Fri)

The Last Supper (22:14–38)
Luke says that

> 'when the time came he took his place at table'
> *(22:14)*.

The Last Supper took place immediately the day started at
6.00 pm. There were six different matters discussed at the
meal:

1 The Vow of Abstinence (22:15–19) Jesus told his apostles
that he had been longing to eat the Passover with them
because he would not eat it again until

> 'the time when it finds fulfilment in the kingdom of
> God' *(22:16)*.

These words are normally taken to mean that Jesus is
predicting his own death. This would be the last Passover he
would celebrate on earth. He repeats the vow after he had
passed round a cup of wine. This cup was one of the four
cups used in the Passover celebration and must not be
confused with the cup used at the institution of the
Eucharist.

2 The Institution of the Eucharist (22:19) The account of the
institution of the Eucharist in Luke's Gospel is complicated
by the fact that, in Luke, it has come down to us in two
forms; in some manuscripts as a short account and in others
as a long asccount.

Short account:

> And he took bread, gave thanks, and broke it; and
> he gave it to them, with the words: 'This is my
> body' *(22:19)*.

Long account:

> And he took bread, gave thanks, and broke it; and
> he gave it to them, with the words: 'This is my
> body **which is given for you; do this as a memorial
> of me.' In the same way he took the cup after
> supper, and said, 'This cup, poured out for you, is
> the new covenant sealed by my blood'** *(22:19b–20)*.

The **bold** words in the long account are very similar to the account found in St Paul's letter to the Corinthians (1 Corinthians 11:24–25). It is thought that Luke as well as Paul used an early form of the words of institution. He prefers this form to that available to him in Mark's Gospel.

The problem comes with the short account with its abrupt ending. The one realistic explanation put forward by scholars is that the account was cut short in some copies to protect the Eucharist from misunderstanding. The omitting of words of meaning was meant to confuse those outside Christianity while, at the same time, making little difference to the faithful who already understood.

The importance of the words of Institution for Christians today

These verses are very important to Christians today. They are central to the celebration of the Eucharist.

This is my body, which is given for you ... This cup, poured out for you, is the new covenant sealed by my blood

This is the language of sacrifice. The breaking of bread and the pouring of wine symbolises the death of Jesus. Christians believe that through the death of Jesus a new relationship is made between God and his people. This relationship is called the 'covenant'. As the Jews remembered the Passover, the Exodus, the time of God's deliverance of his people from their slavery in Egypt, so Christians see, in the Eucharist, God's deliverance of his people from sin. A new relationship with God is possible through the death and resurrection of Jesus.

3   The Betrayal of Judas Foretold (22:21–23) (see notes on 22:3–6)

4   Who is the Greatest? (22:24–30) Luke states that while the meal was going on, the disciples entered into an argument about which one of them was the greatest. Jesus took the opportunity to teach them the true nature of discipleship. It is one of service to others. Jesus has come as a servant,

yet here am I among you like a servant' (22:27).

Jesus then went on to give the reverse side of the argument. There will come a time when Jesus would rule over his kingdom. The disciples are promised a share in that reign.

The word 'judges' (22:30) means 'ruling' in this context. Luke did not mean that the disciples would rule over the Jews. In all probability, he meant, by the phrase, 'the twelve tribes of Israel' (22:30), the 'new Israel', identified as the Christian Church.

5 The Forecast of Peter's Denial (22:31–34) Jesus turned to Simon Peter and told him that the time was near when he would be betrayed by him. Satan would tempt them all. Later on, Peter would recover and be a source of strength to the other disciples. This recovery of Peter is not found in the Gospel but Luke writes how Peter became this source of strength in the early chapters of his second book, The Acts of the Apostles.

Peter said he was ready to die. He would not deny Jesus. Jesus forecast that before the cock crew, Peter would have denied him three times. It was forbidden to keep cockerels within the city of Jerusalem so in all probability, the 'cock crew' was an early morning 'watch' of the Roman day, perhaps a trumpet call.

6 A Time of Crisis (22:35–38) The Last Supper ended with a reference to an event that happened earlier in the Gospel, the mission of the Twelve (9:1–6). At that time they had been sent out in peaceful conditions. Now the situation had changed. The disciples must be ready for any situation. Jesus was now thought of as a criminal (22:37). He wished to know if they are ready for such a change of fortune. They must now have money and a haversack and if necessary sell their cloaks and buy swords.

When Jesus advised the disciples to arm themselves, it is very unlikely that he meant this literally, for it would be completely contrary to his way of life and teaching. The disciples seemed to take it literally for they produced two swords between them. Jesus, aware that they had misunderstood, closed the conversation with the sharp comment,

Enough, enough! (22:38).

The Mount of Olives (22:39–46)
After the Passover meal was finished, Jesus and his disciples went to the Mount of Olives, as they had done every night since arriving in Jerusalem. Luke, unlike Mark and Matthew, does not call the place Gethsemane, although he obviously means the same place. The disciples are told to pray while

Jesus went a little further on to pray himself. The humanity of Jesus is seen in the prayer he offers to God.

> Father, if it be thy will, take this cup away from me.
> Yet not my will but thine be done (22.42).

The 'cup' stood for suffering and Jesus was aware that suffering lay ahead and he was frightened. He prayed to be released but only if it was God's will. Luke, alone, mentions the fact that an angel ministered to Jesus as he prayed so earnestly that his sweat fell to the ground like drops of blood (22:43–44). These verses do not appear in all manuscripts and there is some doubt as to whether they were originally part of the Gospel.

When Jesus returned to the disciples he found them sleeping, worn out by the events of the evening. He woke them up and urged them to continue to pray but it was too late. Judas arrived. Betrayal was at hand.

The Arrest of Jesus (22:47–53)
Judas went up to Jesus to greet him in the usual way with a kiss but Jesus would not let him.

> Judas, would you betray the Son of Man with a
> kiss? (22:48).

Jesus was arrested and in the struggle that followed, the right ear of the High Priest's servant was severed. Luke is the only Gospel who has Jesus healing the man's ear with a touch. It is doubtful if this story is authentic. Jesus would hardly be in a position to carry out this miracle of healing. This detail could well have been added in the passing on of the tradition.

Jesus was arrested by the Temple police, acting on the instructions of the chief priests. He asked them why they had come to do this in secret when he had been available in the Temple each day. Luke interprets the event as the work of evil.

> this is your moment – the hour when darkness
> reigns (22:53).

The Denial of Peter (22:54–65)
Jesus was taken to the High Priest's house and Peter followed, at a distance, right into the courtyard of the house. As he sat there, he was accused three times of being one of

Jesus' men and three times he denied it. After the third time,
the cock crew.

> Jesus turned and looked at Peter. And Peter
> remembered . . . (22:61).

Luke records that while Peter was denying him, Jesus was
being abused both physically and mentally. His guards,
having blindfolded him, were beating him and asking him
which of them it was who had hit him (22:63–65).

The Trial Before the Sanhedrin (22:66–23:1)
The account of the trial of Jesus before the Sanhedrin is a
confused one. It is built, by Luke, on three important titles
given to Jesus (see Chapter 9).

> Are you the Messiah?

Jesus replies that

> from now on, the Son of Man will be seated at the
> right hand of Almighty God.

> You are the Son of God, then?' (22:67–70).

It would seem that the Sanhedrin are intent on asking Jesus
two questions and that Jesus' reply should be looked at as
being separate, as it is impossible to see a logical pattern
running through the three titles in the way Luke uses them.
The use of the title, 'Son of Man' does not lead, naturally, to
the thought that Jesus is claiming to be Son of God. Jesus'
reply to the second question is the one that leads to his
condemnation:

> 'It is you who say I am' or 'You are right, for I am'
> (22:70).

As far as the Sanhedrin is concerned, this is blasphemy
spoken by Jesus and the penalty, according to Jewish law is
death.

The Trial Before Pilate (23:2–25)
Pontius Pilate was the Governor of Judaea from 26 to 36 AD.
The picture of him presented by the New Testament is much
kinder than history remembers him. All the Gospels show
him to be reluctant to condemn Jesus. This is understandable,
in view of the fact that the Gospels were written at a time
when the Church had to exist in a Roman world. It was also
the intention of the Evangelists to blame the Jews as much as

possible for the death of Jesus. Luke seems totally dedicated
to this view of the events. He goes out of his way to
exonerate Pilate and blame the Jews.

- The charges brought by the Sanhedrin have been changed
  from the religious charge of blasphemy to three political
  charges. This casts doubts on the integrity of the Jewish
  leaders. Luke is saying that they purposely change the
  charges in order to stand more chance of having Jesus put
  to death. The three charges were:

  (i) 'subverting the nation'
  (ii) 'opposing taxes to Caesar'
  (iii) 'claiming to be an anointed king'.

  There were serious political charges of inciting people to
  revolt and treason. They carried the death penalty.

- Luke stresses that Pilate tried hard to release Jesus. Three
  times he declares that there is no case for Jesus to answer.
  He is innocent (23:4, 14, 22).
- Luke is the writer to include the story about Jesus being
  sent to Herod Antipas, on the grounds that Jesus was
  from Galilee, the territory governed by Herod. This is not
  really a further trial. Herod mocks Jesus and Jesus remains
  completely silent. The whole episode is something of a
  farce and shows Herod in a poor light.
- At the end of the account, Pilate, at last, gave in to the
  demands of the Jewish leaders and handed Jesus over to
  them. The most probable reason was that he was afraid of
  a riot breaking out in the crowded capital during the
  Passover festivities. Such trouble might well result in a recall to Rome. Such an event had happened by the time
  the Gospel was written. Pilate's only crime was one of
  weakness. Luke makes it clear that the Jews are to blame.
  Although history records that the Romans executed Jesus,
  Luke seems to be saying that even this event was carried
  out by the Jews (23:25–26).

The Crucifixion
The Way of the Cross (23:26–31) Luke records that Simon of
Cyrene was forced into carrying the cross for Jesus but then
goes on to give an account of the journey on the way to
Golgotha. He was followed by a great crowd, which included
some women who wept for him. He told them not to weep
for him but for themselves because the day would arrive

when they would receive enough troubles of their own. This is, most probably, a reference to the coming destruction of Jerusalem in 70 AD.

This passage ends with a difficult verse:

> For if these things are done when the wood is
> green, what will happen when it is dry? (23:31).

There are two possible ways to interpret the saying.

1   If the verse applies to Jesus himself, then it could mean that if this is what befalls the innocent man, what will be the punishment of the guilty?
2   If the saying applies to those lamenting on the way to the cross, then it could mean that they should save their tears for the terrible time ahead when the Romans would crush them.

The Crucifixion (23:32–34) When they reached the place of the skull (in Hebrew, Golgotha), Jesus was crucified with two other criminals, one either side. Even though Luke does not specifically state it, crucifixion involved the nailing of Jesus by his wrists to the cross beam before it was hoisted up and fixed in the permanent upright of the cross. His feet were also nailed. The body was supported by a small block of wood at the bottom of the spine. Crucifixion was a slow painful death by suffocation, the prisoner alternating between pushing himself upright in order to breathe and sagging back to rest and so relieve the intense pain.

As Jesus was crucified he spoke the first of three sentences from the cross, as recorded by Luke.

> Father, forgive them; they do not know what they
> are doing (23:34).

For whom is Jesus asking God's forgiveness? There are three possible alternatives:

1   The Jewish leaders who had brought him before Pilate and secured his execution.
2   The Roman soldiers who had just crucified him.
3   The whole of humanity, who had refused to listen to him, or recognise that he was the person sent by God to bring all people back to himself.

The Mocking of Jesus on the Cross (23:35–38) Luke tells us that the soldiers divided Jesus' clothing, casting lots to see what each should get. This may well be a reference to Psalm 22:18.

In Luke Jesus is mocked by:
– the Jewish leaders;
– the Roman soldiers; and
– one of the criminals crucified with him.

The mockery consisted of the major taunt: that Jesus should save himself because he was:
– the Messiah, the Chosen One and,
– the King of the Jews.

The Two Criminals Executed with Jesus (23:39–43) One of the criminals crucified with Jesus began to taunt him, saying that he should save all three of them. The other criminal rebuked him, recognising the innocence of Jesus. He asked Jesus to remember him and Jesus spoke the second sentence from the cross.

Today you shall be with me in Paradise *(23:43)*.

Paradise was the word used for the Garden of Eden. It stood for a 'state of blessedness' reserved for the good prior to the resurrection at the last day.

The Death of Jesus (23:44–49) The account of Jesus' death in Luke's Gospel begins with the comment about a 'darkness' falling over the whole land from midday until three in the afternoon. Luke, alone, adds the comment about the sun's light failing.

Various suggestions have been made about the meaning of this darkness. It has been suggested that an eclipse of the sun took place. Another suggestion is that it was the fulfilment of a prophecy such as 'I will make the sun go down at noon and darken the earth in broad daylight' (Amos 8:9).

Luke records that the curtain of the Temple was torn in two. This curtain covered the entrance to the Holy of Holies in the Temple. The Jews believed the Holy of Holies was the place where God was to be found. This tearing of the Temple curtain symbolised that the God who was hidden is now revealed to all people. The old religion of Judaism was about to be replaced.

Jesus died, uttering the words,

Father, into your hand I commit my spirit *(23:46)*.

These words are a quotation from Psalm 31:5. The life of Jesus was over. He returned his spirit to God:

that same spirit which had brought him into the world (*1:34–35*).

that same spirit which he had received at baptism (*3:22*).

that same spirit with which he had been anointed at the beginning of his ministry (*4:18–19*).

Luke's story closes with the centurion pronouncing his innocence:

Beyond all doubt this man was innocent (*23:47*).

The Burial (23:50–56)
Luke records that all the friends of Jesus, including the women who had followed him in Galilee, had witnessed the crucifixion. This is in direct contrast to Mark who said that the disciples had deserted Jesus at the moment of arrest and take no further part in the story.

Joseph of Arimathaea, a member of the Sanhedrin, who was obviously sympathetic to Jesus, went to Pilate and asked for the body of Jesus. Joseph

looked forward to the coming of the kingdom of God (*23:51*).

This means that Joseph longed for the coming of the Messiah. Jesus was taken by Joseph and laid to rest in a new tomb. The women took note of where the body of Jesus had been placed. Then they went home to prepare spices with which to anoint the body, once the Sabbath was over.

This story emphasises two points:

1   Jesus was really dead; and
2   It was certain where he had been buried.

This was important to the early Christians because two of the early charges the Christian Church had to face were that Jesus did not really die and that the women went to the wrong tomb on the Sunday morning.

To Answer the Question 'Why Did Jesus Have To Die?'

(a) Luke insists that the death of Jesus was inevitable. It was part of God's plan. The evidence for this is found in the

Gospel. The Son of Man has to suffer (2:34; 9:22; 9:44; 18:31–33; 22:21; 24:; 24:46).

(b) Jesus died because he accepted his mission and was obedient to it. He is the one who

> set his face resolutely towards Jerusalem (*9:51*).

(c) Jesus died because he was rejected by the people, especially the Jewish leaders. They refuse to accept him as Messiah. They reject his authority (5:21; 5:35; 6:11; 7:34; 11:15; 13:33; 22:2; 22:5).

(d) Jesus died because that was the way he could be glorified (24:26).

(e) Jesus died so that repentance and forgiveness of sins could be offered to all people (24:47).

These are the main ideas in Luke's view of the death of Jesus. It is in these ways that he tries to answer the question 'Why did Jesus have to die?'.

What does the death of Jesus mean for Christians today?

The suffering of Jesus was inevitable

While Christians see the suffering of Jesus as part of the human experience that most people go through to some extent or another, they also see the suffering of Jesus as inevitable in a special way. He suffered opposition, rejection and death because of who he was, what he taught, and what he did. They see it as inevitable because he was totally obedient to God. This obedience resulted in death because of the wickedness and sin of humanity.

Reconciliation

Luke portrays Jesus as the perfect man. Christians believe that God sent Jesus to show all people how to live, and thereby, be reconciled to God. Reconciliation means coming back to God and living in harmony with him.

There have been different theories about how this coming back to God works. Not all of them are acceptable to all modern day Christians.

(a) **God must be satisfied** *For some Christians in the Middle Ages and even for some today, the idea of reconciliation was based on the idea that God was offended by the sins of humanity. God, therefore, decided a punishment was necessary. Humanity must pay a debt to God. This debt was only possible if it was made by a perfect person. So God sent his son as the victim who would satisfy God's sense of justice.*

There are many Christians today who find such a theory distasteful. They do not believe in a God who is harsh, unforgiving, willing to inflict pain or needs to be satisfied like some cruel tyrant.

(b) **The Ransom Theory** *Again, in the Middle Ages especially, the theory was that Jesus paid the price to God so that he would free humanity from sin. Jesus was the ransom demanded.*

It is not surprising that most Christians today find this theory totally unacceptable. If God is perfect in his love and mercy, he does not and cannot need a ransom to be paid in order to allow people to come back to him. His nature is not fickle. Perfect love and perfect mercy make no such demands.

The only way a 'ransom' theory makes any sense today, for most Christians, is to understand the word 'ransom' as meaning 'belonging to God'. Then the idea that God showed such a great love for people that he even allowed Jesus to die on the cross in order that his love might persuade them to return to him can make sense. Many Christians, however, would question the value of using the word 'ransom' in this context.

(c) **Jesus the Sacrifice** *At the Last Supper, Jesus said:*

> This cup, poured out for you, is the new covenant
> sealed by my blood (22:20).

This verse is very important in understanding the Christian view of the death of Jesus. The 'blood of the covenant' is a reference to the time of Moses. In those days, an animal was offered in sacrifice to God and its blood was sprinkled over the people as a sign of the one blood or life shared between God and Israel. Many Christians, while they do not see the death of Jesus in the same light, that is, giving his blood to a demanding Father who is out for blood, they do understand Jesus to be making a sacrifice by giving his blood. This sacrifice is the one of giving himself to all people. It is his gift. Through him people are now linked with God in the one life, the life of the covenant. They have entered into an agreement with God.

Luke speaks of a new covenant. This is a reference to Jeremiah 31:31, where the prophet speaks about the agreement made with God will be written on peoples' hearts. The agreement will be an affair of the heart. It will not be just blind obedience to the law out of fear.

(d) **Death and Resurrection** *Some Christians believe that the real meaning of the death of Jesus can only be discovered when linked to the resurrection. Without the resurrection they do not see how the death of Jesus achieves anything. This seems to be what Luke himself says throughout his story of the resurrection.*

> Was the Messiah not bound to suffer thus before entering upon his glory (24:26);

and:

> . . . the Messiah is to suffer death and to rise from the dead on the third day, and that in his name repentance bringing the forgiveness of sins is to be proclaimed to all nations (24:46–7).

Christians see the power of God's love as so strong that it overcomes the sin and wickedness of people who could crucify his son. This power of God also overcomes death. God refused to allow the perfect man to die and by raising him from the dead, wishes the whole of humanity to be reconciled to him.

Study Skills

Knowledge

1 What instructions did Jesus give for the preparations of the Passover?
2 Give an account of what happened at the Passover meal as recorded by Luke.
3 What happened on the Mount of Olives after the Passover meal when Jesus went to pray?
4 What did Jesus say to Judas when he arrived with the crowd to arrest Jesus?
5 Why did the Lord turn and look at Peter?
6 Why did Jesus deserve to die according to Jewish law?
7 Who was the Roman Governor at this time?
8 What charges about Jesus were brought to the Roman Governor by the Jewish leaders?
9 Why did the Roman Governor send Jesus to Herod?
10 Who carried Jesus' cross?

11 What did Jesus say as he was crucified?
12 What did Jesus say to one of the thieves executed with him?
13 What did Jesus say as he died?
14 Who watched at the crucifixion?
15 Who asked for the body of Jesus and buried it in the tomb?

Understanding

16 Do you think the last supper was a Passover meal? Give reasons for your answer.
17 What do you understand Jesus to mean by the words he spoke on the cross in Luke's account of the crucifixion?

Evaluation

18 'Pilate did not want to condemn Jesus'. Explain how and why Luke tries to excuse Pilate from the blame for Jesus' death.
19 'If Jesus had not been crucified there would have been no Christianity'. Do you agree with this statement? Give reasons for your answer.
20 Assess the various beliefs held by Christians about the death of Jesus.

Practical Work

- Find out how the different Christian churches celebrate Holy Week. Try to discover the emphasis they place on the crucifixion. This could be done by inviting representatives of the Churches into school or by interviewing them outside of school.
- Design a wall chart showing the Jerusalem ministry of Jesus as Luke records it. Include an inset showing the ground plan of Jerusalem and the immediate surroundings at that time.

8 The Resurrection of Jesus in Luke's Gospel

The purpose of this chapter is to try to discover what it means for Luke to say 'Jesus is risen'. There are two important questions to be discussed:

- What did the Resurrection mean to Luke?
1 The empty tomb (24:1–12)
2 The road to Emmaus (24:13–15)
3 The apologetic legend (24:36–43)
4 Last instructions to the apostles (24:44–49)
5 The Ascension (24:50–53)
- What does the resurrection mean for Christians today

What did the Resurrection mean to Luke?

The Empty Tomb (24:1–12)

In common with all the Gospels, Luke begins his account of the resurrection with the story of the empty tomb. He records how Mary of Magdala, Joanna, Mary the mother of James and other women went to the tomb, early on the Sunday morning, taking with them spices, presumably to anoint the body of Jesus.

When they arrived they found the stone which had been placed in front of the tomb had been rolled away. When they entered they found two men 'in dazzling garments', who gave to them the message of resurrection.

> 'Why search among the dead for one who lives? He is not here: he has been raised. Remember how he told you while he was still in Galilee, about the Son of Man: how he must be given up into the power of sinful men and be crucified, and must rise again on the third day (24:5–7).

The women returned to the eleven apostles and told them what had happened but they thought it was nonsense. They would not believe them. Luke records that Peter went running to the tomb to see for himself. He found nothing but the wrappings and returned home amazed.

Meaning
The main teaching of this story of the empty tomb is found in the words of the two men. It is a teaching that is expressed simply, yet for Christians, is at the very centre of their faith. Jesus is risen. He had died on the cross on Friday but now he had risen from the dead.

The Road to Emmaus (24:13–35)

Two disciples, one of whom is called Cleopas, were on their way to the village of Emmaus when Jesus met them on the road. They did not recognise him. As they talked they explained that the man, Jesus of Nazareth, whom they had hoped would be the one to 'liberate Israel' had been crucified. They were confused as some women had said that the tomb was empty and that a vision of angels had announced that he was alive. Some of the disciples had visited the tomb and also found it to be empty.

Jesus rebuked the two disciples and began to teach them how the scriptures said that the Messiah had to suffer before he could be glorified.

When they reached Emmaus the two men invited Jesus to stay with them. As Jesus blessed and broke the bread at supper they recognised him but he disappeared from sight. They returned immediately to Jerusalem and told the Eleven, only to find out that Jesus had already appeared to Simon Peter and that the disciples now believed that the resurrection had taken place.

Meaning
This story appears only in Luke. How much of the story is historical and how much it has been developed is difficult to ascertain. For many people there is one main difficulty with the story.

- Why did the two disciples not recognise Jesus? The story says that 'something kept them from seeing who it was'. This is a little unsatisfying and presents problems. It is outside normal human experience.
  The problem of not recognising Jesus becomes even more difficult set against the long conversation held between Jesus and the two others.

Some scholars have suggested that whereas the story of the road to Emmaus may have its foundation in a historical setting, the story has been developed either within the period of oral tradition, or by Luke himself, in order to teach important truths about the resurrection.

There are four such truths:

(a) The appearance of the risen Jesus to Simon Peter The story mentions that Jesus appeared first to Simon Peter. This agrees with the early tradition found in the first letter of Paul to Corinth (1 Cor. 15:3). It may be that the reference to Peter has been added to this story in order to give support to this tradition. Certainly there is no other account of a first appearance to Peter in any of the Gospels.

(b) Jesus was to suffer in order to enter his glory This is a major theme of Luke's Gospel. He sees the suffering of Jesus as a necessary prelude to the glory of the resurrection. Through the Gospel he refers to this (See 9:22; 18:31–33; 24:7; 24:46).

(c) Jesus was the fulfilment of scripture Once again, this is a favourite theme of Luke. He sees Jesus as being the fulfilment of the scriptures. For example, the infancy narratives follow this theme throughout (ch. 1–2); the ministry of Jesus begins with Jesus claiming to fulfil the prophecy of Isaiah (4:18–19) and the whole theme of suffering (9:22; 18:31–33; 24:7) is seen as being the fulfilment of the Old Testament.

(d) Jesus is recognised in the breaking of bread Jesus is recognised at the moment he breaks and blesses the bread. The non-recognition now makes sense. What Luke is saying is that every time bread is broken, then Jesus can and will be recognised.

Most scholars are of the opinion that Luke is suggesting a link between the risen Christ and the eucharist. If this suggestion is correct then of course the story cannot be completely historical. The last supper had only taken place a little over forty-eight hours earlier and therefore, the Eucharist had not yet become an established part of Christianity.

The truth of the story, however, remains. Many Christians believe that Jesus is present in the breaking of the eucharistic bread. There he can be recognised and this happens because he has risen from the dead.

The Apologetic Legend (24:36–43)

Whilst the Eleven and the rest of the company were still discussing the matter of resurrection, Jesus appeared to them. They were afraid because they thought they were seeing a ghost. At first, this seems a little strange in view of their conversation about resurrection but was a perfectly natural reaction when faced with the presence of Jesus.

Jesus, in order to calm them, shows them his hands and feet and invites them to touch him. They were still unconvinced. So Jesus asked for something to eat and was given a piece of grilled fish which he ate in front of them.

Meaning

This passage is known as an Apologetic Legend. This does not mean that what Luke says did not take place. What it means is that Luke has written the event with one purpose in mind and that is to convince his readers that Jesus rose from the dead, in bodily form. It was a physical resurrection.

Luke was writing for the Gentiles of the Roman Empire, who were greatly influenced by Greek culture. He did not want his readers assuming that Jesus had risen in the sense that any good man might be given a place with the gods, which was what the Greeks believed. He wanted his readers to see that the resurrection of Jesus meant that he had returned in a physical form.

Last Instructions to the Apostles (24:44–49)

First of all, Luke returns to the themes already dealt with in the section on the road to Emmaus.

Jesus now instructed the whole of his company as he had done Cleopas and his friend.

(a) Jesus is the fulfilment of scripture.
(b) The Messiah must suffer and rise again.

Secondly, Jesus went on to give the reason for this. All this had happened so that repentance for the forgiveness of sins might be preached to all nations, beginning from Jerusalem. He told them to stay in the city until they were given the power from above (24:49).

Meaning
This is the climax of Luke's Gospel. All that has gone before
leads to this point. Now the work of Jesus is completed, his
followers must take over and begin their mission to the
world. That mission was one of offering repentance that
would bring forgiveness and reconciliation to God. This must
be offered to all nations and they must be the witnesses to it.

This mission would start in Jerusalem. This is very
important to Luke. Throughout his Gospel all things have
pointed towards Jerusalem as the place where the Christ
must go, suffer and die, in order to rise from the dead and
be glorified. Now, beginning from Jerusalem and moving out,
the message of the Christ would be preached to all. The
missionary expansion of Christianity would begin in
Jerusalem (see Chapter 1).

Finally, those who were to begin the mission of
Christianity were not to be left to their own devices. They
were to receive the gift of the Holy Spirit. They were to stay
in the city until they received this gift.

Luke records, in his second book, the Acts of the Apostles,
how the Holy Spirit was given to the Apostles and how the
spread of Christianity began in Jerusalem and later,
throughout the Empire to Rome itself.

The Ascension (24:50–53)

The Gospel concludes with an account of the Ascension.
Jesus and his followers went out to Bethany, a village some
seven miles from Jerusalem. After blessing them he was
parted from them and was carried up to heaven. The
disciples returned to Jerusalem with joy, praising God.

Meaning
The Ascension is a story which is intended to explain how
Jesus, his work on earth complete, returned to be with God.
The people of that time believed that God was in heaven and
that heaven was above the clouds. It was natural, therefore,
for Jesus to ascend in order to return to God. Some
Christians take the account literally. Others see it as a truth
expressed in legendary terms.

SUMMARY

- Luke begins his account of the resurrection with the story of the empty tomb, as do all the Evangelists. The message of the resurrection is delivered to the women at the tomb.
- Jesus appears to two disciples on the Emmaus road. This account teaches:

  1 Jesus had already appeared to Peter
  2 Jesus, as Messiah had to suffer to 'enter his glory' and rise from the dead.
  3 Jesus is the fulfilment of all Jewish scripture.
  4 Jesus is recognised (present) in the breaking of the bread at the eucharist.
- Luke stresses the fact that the resurrection does not mean that Jesus is a ghost. He rose physically in bodily form.
- Jesus instructs the disciples to remain in Jerusalem until they receive the Holy Spirit. Then they are to begin the mission of preaching repentance and forgiveness to all people.
- Jesus returns to be with God at the acension.

What does the Resurrection mean for Christians today?

Christians accept that there is no historical evidence for the resurrection other than the fact that the disciples believed it happened. They accept that nobody witnessed the actual resurrection itself. Yet Christianity stands or falls with the resurrection. As Paul says in his first letter to the Church at Corinth:

> *If there is no resurrection, then Christ was not raised; and if Christ was not raised, then our Gospel is null and void, and so is your faith . . . (1 Cor. 15:14).*

What about the empty tomb?

The only story about the resurrection that occurs in all the Gospels is the one about the empty tomb. It is freely accepted by

Christians that the fact that the tomb was empty proves nothing in itself.

The question of the empty tomb has been surrounded by argument since the earliest days of Christianity. Many theories have been put forward to explain why the tomb was empty and to discredit Christianity.

1 *Jesus was not really dead and revived in the cool of the tomb.*
2 *The women went to the wrong tomb.*
3 *Someone stole the body of Jesus. There are only three groups who could have done this; the disciples, the Jewish leaders or the Roman authorities.*

The trouble with these different theories is that, even for a lot of non-Christians, they make little sense. It is difficult to imagine anyone surviving death by crucifixion. If the women went to the wrong tomb, it is highly unlikely that someone would not have checked when the rumours started to circulate. Indeed, Luke records that Peter did go to see for himself. This theory would only begin to make sense if we accept the fact that he too went to the wrong tomb.

There seems to be no sensible reason why anyone would have stolen the body of Jesus. If the disciples did it, then it would mean that the whole of Christianity is based on a lie. It is difficult to accept that the disciples would live this lie to the extent of even dying for their so-called faith in resurrection. If either the Jewish leaders or the Roman authorities had stolen the body, why did they not produce the evidence when the disciples began to preach that Jesus had risen from the dead?

Such theories do not trouble Christians today, not just because they do not believe them, but because their faith is not based simply on the fact of the empty tomb. They believe in the resurrection. The story of the empty tomb is secondary. It is the resurrection that makes sense of the empty tomb and not the empty tomb that proves resurrection.

Did the Resurrection happen?

- *Christians believe that something happened after the Resurrection.*
- *They believe this not just because there are stories in the Gospels about Jesus appearing to his disciples.*
- *There is another reason. The existence of the Christian Church is based on the Resurrection. Something happened to transform that group of hopeless, frightened men into men of*

courage, who now spoke boldly in public and were prepared to die for their new-found belief.

- *The disciples themselves gave the reason for this change of attitude. They were convinced Jesus was alive and with them. Luke records, in the Acts of the Apostles, the beginnings of the Christian Church. He shows that every time the disciples preached the message was the same.*

> *The Jesus we speak of has been raised by God, as we can all bear witness (Acts 2:32).*

(see also Acts 3:26; 4:10; 5:31; 10:40; 13:30; 17:31)

It would appear that the existence of the Christian Church is due to the conviction that Jesus had risen from the dead.

What happened?

It is impossible to say what happened at the moment of resurrection. Christians, therefore, differ in their assumptions of what took place.

- *Some Christians have suggested that the resurrection did not happen to Jesus at all. They claim that the disciples became aware of who Jesus was and what he had come to do, only after his death and were inspired to carry on his work. This has happened many times in history. Followers of great men and women have carried on their work long after their death, inspired by their leadership and beliefs.*

  Such a view, however, ignores the accounts of the empty tomb and the resurrection appearances. Nor does it explain the extraordinary change that came over the Apostles. It is difficult for many Christians to see how the disciples suddenly believed in resurrection, expressed it in the way they did and began the process of building Christianity on what was after all, an untruth.

- *Other Christians believe that Jesus rose from the dead in bodily form. They accept what Luke says. He was not a ghost and could be touched and could eat (24:41–43). They see a firm link between the Jesus who had lived with his disciples and the risen Lord. Jesus was dead but had been brought back to life.*

  The main weakness with this point of view is that it ignores some of the other evidence found in the Gospels. It oversimplifies the mystery of resurrection and reduces it to the idea of a corpse coming back to life.

- *A third view, held by many Christians, accepts the bodily resurrection of Jesus but also allows for other matters to be taken into consideration. The resurrection was not just a corpse coming back to life. There was something different about the risen Jesus. The disciples, for example, sometimes doubted (24:42); Jesus seemed able to come and go as he pleased in a way that was not normal (24:31; John 20:19, 26). Above all he is recognised, accepted and worshipped in faith. Even for the first Christians, faith was the only way to a full understanding of the risen Christ.*

What does the Resurrection mean?

- *Christians believe the Resurrection proves the identity of Jesus. He is, without doubt,*

  - *the SAVIOUR*
  - *the CHRIST of GOD;*
  - *the SON OF MAN;*
  - *the SON OF GOD;*
  - *the LORD*

  (see Chapter 9)

  A Christian is one who confesses Jesus is LORD.
- *Christians believe the resurrection confirms the work of Jesus. His life and death were an attempt to bring all people back to God. God has confirmed this work by raising Jesus from the dead. Through the resurrection, forgiveness of sins can take place (24:47) and people can be restored to God. Jesus had to suffer to enter glory (24:26).*
- *Christians believe that the resurrection means something in everyday experience. It is not just an event of the past but has meaning for the present. They believe Jesus is alive and with them today and can be experienced in daily life. Many of them also believe that he is especially present with them in the bread broken at the eucharist. It is there that they recognise him (24:31).*
- *Christians believe that the resurrection means that death has been overcome. Jesus has triumphed over death. For his followers, death is not the end but the beginning of eternal life that already exists in the relationship enjoyed with the risen Jesus here and now.*

Study Skills

Knowledge

1 Who went to the tomb early on the Sunday morning?
2 Why did they go to the tomb?
3 What was the message of the two men in the tomb?
4 Where were Cleopas and his companion going when they met Jesus?
5 According to Luke, why didn't they recognise Jesus?
6 When did they recognise Jesus?
7 Who, according to Luke, saw the risen Jesus first?
8 How did Jesus prove he was not a ghost when he appeared to the Eleven?
9 What did Jesus say the disciples had to do?
10 What special gift did Jesus promise to send the disciples?
11 Where would they receive this gift?
12 Where did the ascension take place in Luke's Gospel?

Understanding

13 What do you think Luke is trying to teach about the risen Jesus in the story of the two disciples on the road to Emmaus?
14 Explain the words:
'. . . in his name repentance bringing the forgiveness of sins is to be proclaimed to all nations. Begin in Jerusalem; it is you who are witnesses to it all . . . so stay in the city until you are armed with the power from above' (24:47–49).

Evaluation

15 How important do you think belief in the empty tomb is to an understanding of resurrection?
16 Explain one difficulty a person might have in believing the resurrection. How might you answer that difficulty?

Examination Practice

Give a careful account of Luke's story of the empty tomb.   (6)
Why do you think the disciples did not believe the message the women told them when they returned from the tomb?   (5)
Outline briefly one other story about resurrection in Luke's Gospel.   (4)
What do Christians believe about resurrection?   (5)

Practical Work

- In small groups, work out three simple questions on the resurrection. Each member of the group should then interview one or two adult Christians on the basis of the three questions. Then, in your groups, compile the results of the survey into belief in the resurrection.

9 Who is Jesus?

The purpose of this chapter is to discover who Luke thinks Jesus is. This also gives an insight into the belief of the first century Christians about the person of Jesus.

This can be done by examining the following:

– The title Jesus uses of himself
– Other titles used of Jesus

1   Messiah
2   Son of God
3   Saviour
4   Lord

The Title Jesus uses of himself

Son of Man

This is the title which is only used by Jesus. No one else, not even the author in his editorial narrative, uses it of Jesus. Many scholars believe it to be the most authentic title for this very reason.

Perhaps Jesus called himself by this uncommon name so that he could accomplish his mission to

> seek and save the lost (*19:10*)

without making an open claim to be the Messiah. Such a claim would either have been misunderstood or could even have brought about a speedy end to his ministry.

The title 'Son of Man' has its origin in the Old Testament where there were two distinct ways to interpret the title.

(a) In the earliest Hebrew poetry it simply meant 'a man' or 'man' in general.

> 'What is man that thou shouldst remember him, mortal man (literally Son of Man) that thou shouldst care for him?' (Psalm 8:4).

(b) In the Old Testament book of Daniel, the phrase takes on a special meaning. In Chapter 7 there is an account of one of Daniel's visions. He saw four great beasts appear from the sea. They were savage and terrifying. Then he saw an old man sitting as though in judgment and 'one like a son of man' (Daniel 7:13) was presented to him on 'the clouds of heaven'. He was brought before the old man, honoured by him and given power, glory and sovereignty.

The author of the book of Daniel gives an interpretation of the vision. The beasts stand for the nations such as Babylon who had conquered the Jews, and the figure of the Son of Man represented 'the saints of the Most High'. These were God's loyal few who were ready to suffer and die rather than deny their faith in God. They will be given their place in heaven.

In Luke's Gospel, Jesus seems to use the title 'Son of Man' in both these Old Testament ways.

(a) There are three occasions where Jesus, in speaking of himself, seems to use the title just to mean himself as a man.

1   He uses it to speak of his mission:

the Son of Man has come to seek and save what is lost (19:10).

2   He uses it when commenting on the cost of discipleship:

Foxes have their holes, the birds their roosts; but the Son of Man has nowhere to lay his head (9:58).

3   He uses it when criticising the people for their negative reaction to him:

The Son of Man came eating and drinking, and you say 'Look at him! a glutton and a drinker, a friend of tax-gatherers and sinners!' (7:34).

(b) Luke also has many references that show that Jesus thought of himself as the Son of Man in the Daniel sense. They carry the idea of Jesus being cast in the role of the one who will come in power and glory on 'the clouds of heaven' at the end of time. This second coming of Jesus is called the Parousia.

1   The first reference is from a passage focusing on what it means to be a disciple:

For whoever is ashamed of me and my words, the Son of Man will be ashamed of him, when he comes

in his glory and the glory of the Father and the holy
angels (9:26).

2   The reverse is also true. Later, in the Gospel, Jesus says to
his friends:

everyone who acknowledges me before men, the Son
of Man will acknowledge before the angels of God
(12:8).

3   Later in the same chapter, Jesus tells his disciples to be
ready for the coming of the Son of Man for he will come
unexpectedly:

Hold yourselves ready, then, because the Son of
Man will come at a time you least expect him
(12:40).

4   The Pharisees asked Jesus when the kingdom of God
would come. They were told that it was not possible to
observe the signs of its coming; in fact, it was already
present (17:20–21). Jesus then went on to teach his
disciples about the signs of the coming of the Son of
Man. It will happen suddenly like a flash of lightening:

The time will come when you long to see one of the
days of the Son of Man, but you will not see it . . .
For like the lightening-flash that lights up the earth
from end to end, will the Son of Man be when his
day comes. But first he must endure much suffering
and be repudiated by this generation (17:22–25).

Jesus went on to give two illustrations about the suddenness
of this future event. At the time of Noah, life went on
without thought of danger right up until the time of the
great flood. The same happened in the wicked city of Sodom.
Life went on right up to the day it was destroyed:

it will be like that on the day when the Son of Man
is revealed (17:26–30).

5   The next verse comes from the Apocalyptic passage in
chapter 21. In this Jesus is talking about the signs that
will accompany the end of the world.

> And then they will see the Son of Man coming on
> the cloud with great power and glory (21:27).

A few verses later the disciples are told, once again, to be alert because the timing of the end is a secret. No one knows when it will happen.

> Be on the alert, praying at all times for strength to
> pass safely through all these imminent troubles and
> to stand in the presence of the Son of Man (21:36).

6   The last of the references to the Son of Man, related
    directly to Daniel is at the trial before the Sanhedrin.
    Jesus was asked if he was the Messiah. Jesus does not
    answer this question but tells the Jewish leaders:

> But from now on, the Son of Man will be seated at
> the right hand of Almighty God (22:69).

There are two more Son of Man sayings in Luke's Gospel concerning the question of authority. The Gospel claims that the authority of Jesus came from God, for Jesus claimed to do things that only God can do. In this way he is acting as the divine representative of God in the Daniel sense.

The first is from the healing of the paralysed man (see Chapter 6):

> . . . the Son of Man has the right on earth to forgive
> sins (5:24).

The second is from a passage where Jesus and his disciples are criticised for breaking the Sabbath law (see Chapter 3). Jesus claimed his authority was greater than the Sabbath Law:

> The Son of Man is sovereign even over the Sabbath
> (6:5).

All the other sayings about the Son of Man in Luke deal with the themes of suffering, death and resurrection. This is only a small part of the theme of the book of Daniel. There are six such sayings.

1   The first warns the disciples that they, like Jesus, can
    expect nothing but hatred and suffering:

How blest you are when men hate you, when they outlaw you and insult you, and ban your very name as infamous, because of the Son of Man (*6:22*).

2   After the profession of faith by Peter, Jesus predicted for the first time that he was going to die:

The Son of Man has to undergo great sufferings, and to be rejected by the elders, chief priests, and doctors of the law, to be put to death and to be raised again on the third day (*9:22*).

3   Again, after the transfiguration Jesus warns his disciples:

The Son of Man is to be given up into the power of men (*9:44*).

4   A third time Jesus predicted his impending death:

We are now going up to Jerusalem; and all that was written by the prophets will come true for the Son of Man. He will be handed over to the foreign power. He will be mocked, maltreated, and spat upon. They will flog him and kill him, and on the third day he will rise again (*18:31–33*).

5   At the Last Supper, Jesus tells his disciples:

But mark this – my betrayer is here, his hand with mine on the table. For the Son of Man is going his appointed way . . . (*22:21–22*).

6   Finally, at the resurrection itself, the two men in white, who give the message of resurrection to the women, recall what Jesus had told them previously:

Remember what he told you while he was still in Galilee, about the Son of Man: how he must be given up into the power of sinful men and be crucified, and must rise again on the third day (*24:6–7*).

It is extremely doubtful that the book of Daniel stands behind these sayings of the Son of Man suffering, dying and rising again. There is, however, another Old Testament book where the answer might be found. In Isaiah there is a collection of songs or poems about someone who is known as 'the Servant of the Lord'. These passages are sometimes called 'The Suffering Servant Songs' and the person they refer to, 'The Suffering Servant'. Scholars believe that Jesus combined the idea of the Son of Man from Daniel with the Suffering Servant of Isaiah. In Isaiah 53, for example, the picture of the Servant fits neatly with the words and experience of Jesus. 'He was despised . . . tormented and humbled by suffering; we despised him . . . Yet on himself he bore our sufferings' (Isaiah 53:3–4). His suffering was not of his own making but was a punishment for the sins of others.

This joining of the dual role of the Son of Man of Daniel and the suffering servant of Isaiah is unique in the Gospels. It has no parallel in Jewish literature. Many people think that the person responsible was Jesus himself.

SUMMARY

The title Son of Man is used in three ways in the Gospel of Luke.

1   Jesus uses the title to refer to his own human situation.
2   Jesus uses the title to refer to his return as judge, in power and glory, to set up the rule of God on earth (the theme of Daniel).
3   Jesus uses the title to refer to his suffering, death and resurrection, to save people from their sins (the theme of Isaiah).

Always, this title is used by Jesus and no one else.

Jesus: the Son of Man for today

What relevance does Jesus, as Son of Man, have for people today? This is the most difficult of all the titles of Jesus for twentieth century Christians as they rarely use the title. This is a pity for the title is of great value.

(a) The title 'Son of Man' still speaks to many Christians today, of a time in the future when Jesus will return and assist in judgment.
On the other hand, many people, today, think that judgment is not all that important. Everyone will finally be accepted into heaven for God is a God of love and mercy and he will not turn anyone away.

On the other hand there are those Christians who seem to let the pendulum swing too far the other way and think of God as someone who takes delight in condemnation. They look forward to the time when Jesus will return and exercise judgment on a wicked world.

The truth lies between these two extreme views. The New Testament speaks of both God's mercy and his judgment. It warns of a time when humanity will be faced with judgment. The disciple who is 'ashamed' of Jesus will face the same treatment at the time of judgment (9:26).

(b) This idea of judgement makes sense when placed alongside the suffering of the Son of Man. Jesus suffered, died and rose again to save people from the power of sin. This has always been a fundamental belief of Christians. They believe Jesus came to call all people back to God. This message of God's love was ignored and instead of acceptance, Jesus was rejected and executed. By his death, however, he showed the full extent of God's love. He was willing to die to show people how much God wished them to belong to him. This sacrifice of Jesus, however, is not the end. Three days later he rose from the dead.

Christians believe that a person who responds to this message of the death and resurrection of Jesus can be united with God and will be saved from the power of evil which is called sin. This is what it means to call Jesus 'Son of Man'.

Other Titles Used of Jesus

The Messiah

The title 'Messiah' means 'anointed one'. 'Messiah' is a Hebrew word. In Greek the same word is 'Christ'. It is most important to realise that the words 'Messiah' and 'Christ' are the same word.

> Jesus the Messiah (Hebrew)
> Jesus the Christ (Greek)
> Jesus the Anointed One (English).

All three mean the same.

The background to the title is Jewish. The Jews believed their God was the only God. He was all powerful; he controlled the destiny of all nations and peoples. This high belief was severely tested after Israel had been taken captive by the Babylonians in the sixth century BC.

During the period of exile, the Jews began to hope for the day when a leader would arise who would restore the nation to its former glory. They took to heart once more, the promise of Moses, made a long time ago. 'The Lord your God will raise up a prophet from among you like myself, and you will listen to him' (Deuteronomy 18:15).

The idea of a Messiah figure gradually took shape. The main beliefs about him were:

- He would be the representative of God who would protect the chosen people from all their enemies.
- The holy city of Jerusalem and the holy Temple would become the centre of the world.
- All the chosen people of Israel, wherever they were in the world would be gathered into Palestine.
- The Messiah would establish the rule of God on earth. This would bring about an age of perfect happiness and peace.

This was a magnificent hope but it did not last. By the time of Jesus, this high theology of Messiahship had been watered down into a nationalistic hope for an earthly leader who would fight and drive out the Romans.

When Luke uses this title, he returns, in part, to the high hope of Judaism. Rather than weaken the idea of Messiahship, Luke adds to it and presents Jesus as the Messiah who has come, not just for the Jews, but for all people.

(a) This was the purpose of the coming of Jesus. So at the birth of the baby in Bethlehem, the angel's message to the shepherds in the fields was one of Messiahship.

> Today in the city of David a deliverer has been born to you – the **Messiah**, the Lord (2:11).

(b) This view is supported by Simeon, in the Temple, at the time of Jesus' presentation. Simeon was a devout man who

watched and waited for the restoration of Israel
(2:25)

and had been promised:

he would not see death until he had seen the Lord's
Messiah (2:26).

John the Baptist prepares the way (3:1–20)
(c) Luke begins the ministry of John the Baptist by
attempting to set him in history. The references given are a
little general with the exception of the actual year of the
Roman Emperor's reign.

Fifteenth year of Tiberius	AD 28
Pontius Pilate: Governor of Judaea	AD 26–36
Herod Antipas: Tetrarch of Galilee	4 BC–AD 39
Philip: Tetrarch of Ituraea	
and Trachonitis	4 BC–AD 34
Annas: High Priest	6 BC–AD 15
Caiaphas: High Priest	AD 18–36

It should be noted that although Annas ceased to be High Priest
in AD 15, he had great influence over the members of his family
who succeeded him, the most well-known being Caiaphas. This
influence amounted to full status and powers. At that time John
preached throughout the Jordan valley. He offered the people
baptism as a means of repentance for the forgiveness of sins.
The word repentance means 'to turn around'. In other words,
they were to return to a life free from the sins of injustice and
dishonesty.

The quotation recorded by Luke makes it clear that from the
outset, the theme of universalism is to be emphasised. The new
way was to be open to all peoples, Gentiles as well as Jews.

all mankind shall see God's deliverance (3:6).

The preaching of John was directed against the Jews. No one
can escape the coming wrath of God except those who, by
repenting, change the direction of their lives. Just belonging to
the Jewish nation will not save them for the axe was about to
be laid at the very root of the nation's life.

The ordinary people were to make amends for their past.
They were called on to share their goods. The tax-collectors
were told to stop their extortion and the soldiers were told to
stop bullying people and make do with their rightful wages.

All this led up to the suggestion that John, himself, was the Christ. John heard this rumour and forecast the arrival of the Messiah. The Messiah would come with fire and spirit. He was referring to Jesus. As far as John was concerned, Jesus was the anointed one of God for whom he was preparing the way.

John's violent preaching led to his downfall. He rebuked Herod Antipas for his adulterous relationship with Herodias, the wife of Antipas' half brother Philip. Antipas retaliated by imprisoning John and even though Luke does not record it, John was later beheaded by Herod Antipas.

(d) Unlike the other Gospels, Luke claims that the beginning of Jesus' ministry happened on the Sabbath day in the synagogue of his own village, Nazareth. He was chosen to read the lesson from the book of the prophets. The lesson for that day was from the prophet Isaiah and the words are most significant.

> The Spirit of the Lord is upon me because he has
> **anointed** me;
> he has sent me to announce good news to the poor,
> to proclaim release for prisoners and
> recovery of sight to the blind;
> to let the broken victims go free,
> to proclaim the year of the Lord's favour
> (4:18–19; Isaiah 61:1–2).

Immediately after the lesson, Jesus rose to deliver the homily. His opening words were startling:

> Today, in your very hearing this text has come true
> (4:21).

What Jesus is claiming is that he is the Lord's anointed one; in other words the Messiah. The story goes on to give an indication of the sort of Messiah Jesus would become. At first the words of Jesus were well received but gradually the enthusiasm of the congregation gave way to cynicism as they realised that the speaker was, after all, the son of the local carpenter, Joseph. Jesus, aware of their change of mood, gave two illustrations of his future Messiahship. First of all, he told them the story of Elijah and the widow of Sarepta. In the time of Elijah, there had been a great famine and Elijah found refuge, not amongst the Jews in Israel, but in this town in the Gentile territory of Sidon.

The second illustration was similar. In the prophet Elisha's time, there were many lepers in Israel but the only one Elisha cured was a Gentile called Naaman, from Syria. The congregation were furious with Jesus and hustled him out of the synagogue.

What Jesus was saying by the use of these two illustrations is that his Messiahship is for all people, not just the Jews. The kingdom of God would be set up not just amongst the faithful of the chosen people but amongst all faithful of every nation. This account highlights the theme of universalism found in Luke's Gospel.

John the Baptist's question (7:18–35)
(e) Later in the ministry of Jesus, John the Baptist sent two disciples to ask Jesus a direct question:

> Are you the one who is to come, or are we to expect some other? (*7:19*).

The answer of Jesus, based on the quotation from Isaiah which he read in the synagogue at Nazareth at the beginning of his ministry, makes it clear that Jesus is the **Messiah**.

> Go and tell John what you have seen and heard;
> how the blind recover their sight, the lame walk, the
> lepers are made clean, the deaf hear, the dead are
> raised to life, the poor are hearing the good news –
> and happy is the man who does not find me a
> stumbling-block (*7:22–23*).

This is the role of the **Messiah**.

(f) The only person in the Gospel to recognise Jesus, apart from the evil spirits (4:41), was Peter. In answer to Jesus' question,

> 'Who do you say I am?', Peter said 'God's **Messiah**' (*9:20*).

Jesus gave his disciples strict orders not to tell anyone. The explanation for this command of silence may well have been that Jesus did not want to be thought of as the popular Messianic figure who would drive out the Romans.

(g) No one else even thinks of suggesting that Jesus is the Messiah until the trial of Jesus before the Sanhedrin. Then they ask the question:

Tell us, are you the Messiah? (22:67).

Jesus does not give, in Luke's Gospel, a direct answer to this question. Nevertheless, the Jewish leaders include this charge when they take Jesus to Pilate.

We found this man . . . claiming to be Messiah, a king (23:2).

(h) Two of the references mentioning Jesus as Messiah are heavy with sarcasm. They are the taunts Jesus received, having been crucified:

He saved others: now let him save himself, if this is God's **Messiah**, his chosen (23:35).

Are you the **Messiah**? Save yourself and us (23:39).

(i) Twice, after the resurrection, Jesus admits that he is the **Messiah**. On both occasions he was instructing his disciples, firstly, the two on the Emmaus road, and secondly, the eleven Apostles.

Was not the **Messiah** bound to suffer thus before entering his glory (24:26).

This is what is written: that the **Messiah** is to suffer death and to rise from the dead on the third day, and that in his name repentance bringing the forgiveness of sins is to be proclaimed to all nations (24:46–47).

(j) In addition, there is a rare title used which also indicates the Messiahship of Jesus. The blind man at Jericho calls out,

Jesus, **Son of David**, have pity on me.

It is meant to be understood that Jesus is the Messiah as the Jews believed that the Messiah would be a descendant of King David (1:32).

There is no doubt that through the words and work of Jesus, the early Church came quickly to the belief that Jesus was the Messiah, the Christ of God, the anointed one.

Jesus: the Messiah for today

Just as the Jews believed in a Messiah, who would come bringing peace, and establishing the rule of God on earth, so Christians

today see in Jesus that same Messianic figure who has come and who has, is and will establish God's kingdom on earth. The daily prayer of Christianity includes the phrase, 'Your kingdom come, Your will be done, on earth as it is in heaven'.

The Jews also believed that the Messiah would free them from all their sufferings. Christians see Jesus the Messiah as the one who will lead them, and the whole world, through suffering, and bring them and it back to God.

Christians believe the world today needs this salvation; it is not a happy place because poverty, starvation and violence bring, misery and suffering to thousands.

Christians are committed to joining with the Messiah in not only resisting this evil, but fighting against it. Outstanding examples of this struggle can be found in Christian history. From the twentieth century, names spring to mind like Dr Albert Schweitzer who fought against the misery of leprosy in Africa; Dr Martin Luther King and the struggle for equal rights in America; and Mother Teresa of Calcutta who continues to work in the slums of India doing Messianic work.

It must be stated that while many non-Christian organisations are engaged in the same struggles, it is the absolute duty of the Christian to be committed, with Jesus the Messiah, in this struggle against the evils and injustices of the world; and to work for peace and the coming of God's Messianic kingdom.

The Son of God

Today the title 'Son of God' is the most popular title given to Jesus and it has been so for two thousand years.

The origin of the title is to be found in the Old Testament, where the nation, Israel, is often referred to as God's son. In the prophet Hosea, for example, God says,

> When Israel was a boy, I loved him;
> I called my son out of Egypt (Hosea 11:1).

By the time of Jesus the idea of a representative of God being called the 'Son of God' was seen as a Messianic title. Early in the history of Christianity, it became a title that went beyond that of the Messiah. It expressed the closest possible relationship between God and Jesus. This relationship is seen clearly in Luke's Gospel.

The Birth of Jesus
Even before the birth of Jesus the announcement of his sonship was made by the angel to Mary. The announcement

was not just the fact that she would have a child but that the child would be special to God; born in a special way.

> The Holy Spirit will come upon you, and the power of the Most High (that is: the power of God) will overshadow you; and for that reason the holy child to be born will be called 'Son of God' (1:34–35).

The Baptism of Jesus

The next occasion when the title is used is at the baptism of Jesus. Luke's account is somewhat strange in that it does not actually state that Jesus was baptised by John the Baptist. In fact in the previous paragraph it says that John had been imprisoned by Herod Antipas for criticising his relationship with Herodias, who was married to his half brother. Luke emphasises the part played by the Holy Spirit rather than the baptism itself.

At the moment of baptism, however, Luke describes how the voice of God spoke to Jesus about the close relationship between them.

> Thou art **my Son, the Beloved**; on thee my favour rests (3:22).

These words come from two different parts of the Old Testament.
- 'Thou art my Son, the Beloved' is a quotation based on Psalm 2, a Messianic Psalm that talks about the Messiah coming to reign over Israel.
- 'on Thee my favour rests' is a quotation from the Suffering Servant Songs of Isaiah (see 'Son of Man') (Isaiah 42); and by inference shows that the Messiah will be one who will suffer.

So Jesus is confirmed at one and the same time as both a Messianic figure but also a figure who will experience suffering and he will do this because he is God's Son.

Recognised by Evil

(a) It is interesting that the forces of evil seem to have no difficulty in recognising the person of Jesus in Luke's Gospel. Early in the Gospel Luke records this general summary:

> At sunset all who had friends suffering from one disease or another brought them to him; and he laid his hands on them one by one and cured them. Devils also came out of many of them, shouting,

'You are the Son of God'. But he rebuked them and forbade them to speak, because they knew that he was the Messiah (4:40–41).

(b) Immediately after his baptism, Jesus went out into the wilderness and was tempted by the devil. The story of the three temptations are a way of introducing the ministry of Jesus for they are all to do with the question of how Jesus was to accomplish his mission. Many people believe the best way of interpreting the temptations is to see them as the inner turmoil going on in the mind of Jesus rather than a conversation with the devil in person. The devil stands for the force of evil in the world which all people experience.

1   If you are the **Son of God**, tell this stone to become bread (4:3).

The devil recognised Jesus and tempted him to use his power not only to satisfy his own hunger, but also as a means of persuading people to follow him. Such an appeal would have been for the wrong reasons. Jesus resists the temptation by quoting the Old Testament book of Deuteronomy; 'Man cannot live on bread alone' (4:4; Deuteronomy 8:3).

2   In the second temptation, the devil showed Jesus, 'in a flash', all the kingdoms of the world and promised him total power if he would only do homage and worship him. The Son of God was being tempted to turn his back on God and become an advocate for evil. This was a real temptation for Jesus could have used such powers to have become a powerful world leader. Jesus rejected the temptation because it would have meant turning his back on God.

You shall do homage to the Lord your God and worship him alone (4:8).

3   In the third temptation, Jesus is taken to the parapet of the Temple in Jerusalem.

If you are the **Son of God**, throw yourself down; for Scripture says, 'He will give his angels orders to take care of you' (4:10).

Jesus was tempted to use his powers to perform incredible and magical tricks in order to make people respond to him and accept him. The reply of Jesus was, once again, from the book of Deuteronomy,

> You are not to put the Lord your God to the test
> (4:12; Deuteronomy 6:16).

The Son of God was not to give in to such temptations and
so the devil left him.

It is also interesting that in two separate stories about
exorcism, the evil spirits recognise Jesus as Son of God. They
use, in each case, rare titles which are variants on the Son of
God.

The first is in the story of the Capernaum demoniac. The
possessed man shouts:

> Ha! What do you want with us, Jesus of Nazareth?
> Have you come to destroy us? I know who you are:
> **the Holy One of God** (4:34).

This is very near to calling Jesus the Son of God (see Chapter
5).

The second appears in the story of the Gergesene
demoniac. Legion shouts:

> What do you want with me, Jesus, **Son of the Most
> High God?** (8:28).

In fear Legion calls Jesus by this name which is the same as
calling him the Son of God (1:32) (see Chapter 5).

The Transfiguration
When Jesus, accompanied by Peter, James and John, went up
a mountain to pray, he was seen in a visionary state with
Moses and Elijah. These two men were the holy
representatives of Judaism. Moses was the great leader and
Law-giver; Elijah, the great prophet. Elijah was supposed to
return to prepare the way for the Messiah and in one sense,
the Jews looked for a new Moses. Jesus is seen with both of
them talking about his

> departure, the destiny he was to fulfil in Jerusalem
> (9:31).

This means Jesus' death.

A cloud covered the scene and the voice of God, with
words similar to those used at the baptism, said,

> This is **my Son**, my Chosen; listen to him (9:35).

After this Jesus was found to be alone. Moses and Elijah had disappeared and the focus of attention had switched completely to Jesus. He is the Son of God – so listen to him.

The Father and the Son

In one short sentence, unique in the Synoptic Gospels, Luke records the close relationship between Jesus and God.

> Everything is entrusted to me by my Father; and no one knows who the Son is but the Father, or who the Father is but the Son, and those to whom the Son may choose to reveal him (10:22).

This mutual understanding between Father and Son is thought to be from a separate source and is more like the style found in John's Gospel.

The Parable of the Wicked Husbandmen

> What am I to do? I will send my own dear son; perhaps they will respect him (20:13).

This parable deals with the theme of the salvation history. The son is sent by the owner of the vineyard (God), after all attempts to communicate with the tenants (Jewish leaders), through the servants (prophets) had failed. This was to fail too for the tenants

> flung him out of the vineyard and killed him (20:15).

Once again the parable indicates the close relationship enjoyed between Jesus and God.

Jesus Before the Sanhedrin

The last occasion where Luke records the title is during the trial of Jesus before the Sanhedrin (see Chapter 7).

The Chief Priests and Doctors of the Law asked Jesus:

> You are the **Son of God** then?

to which Jesus replied:

> it is you who say I am (22:70).

This comment was taken by the Jewish leaders to mean, 'yes', and Jesus is condemned for speaking blasphemy:

> We have heard it ourselves from his own lips (22:71).

In summary the meaning of the title in Luke's Gospel is that Jesus is a special person:

- a person in the tradition of the Old Testament
- a person born through the creative power of the Holy Spirit
- a person chosen by God and given a mission
- a person recognised by evil
- a person who had to resist evil
- a person who enjoyed the closest possible relationship with God
- a son, special beyond words

Jesus: the Son of God for today

Many people have difficulty in understanding what God is really like. This is not surprising. God is not a human being. Even when God is called 'Father', it is only an image that is being used. Unlike a human father God is everywhere; he is all-powerful; he is perfect. Such ideas have always been hard for people to understand.

Christians believe Jesus provides the answer to the question, 'What is God really like?'. When they look at Jesus, he is like a window through which they can see God. Jesus is someone ordinary people can understand, yet he mirrors the perfect qualities of God.

For example, God's love for people is shown in the way Jesus cared for those who were sick or outcasts from society such as Zacchaeus (19:1–10); or the woman who was a sinner (7:36–50).

God's desire for all people to come to him is shown in the way Jesus was willing to die to convince them of his love. Christians believe Jesus does this because he is the 'Son of God'.

Saviour

This is the rarest title in the Gospel. It does not occur at all in Matthew and Mark and is found only once in Luke.

> Today in the city of David a **deliverer** (**Saviour**) has been born to you – the Messiah, the Lord (2:11).

The title means that Jesus is seen as the one who can bring people back to God through his life, death and resurrection. Such people are 'saved' from evil and live with God both now and in eternity.

Jesus: Saviour for today

Most Christians believe that humanity is cut off from God. The main problem is human nature which falls far short of the perfection of God. Even when men and women try, by discipline, legalism or good works, to draw near to God, it is doomed to fail. They claim that in Jesus, God has shown his love for all men and women.

This love was rejected and Jesus was killed but God would not allow his love to be blotted out and raised Jesus from the dead. To anyone who receives the Christian faith, he offers salvation. Salvation is not something to be earned. It is not a reward. It is a free gift of God.

Some Christians claim that God's free gift must apply to all and that means everybody will be saved in the end. Others point out that while the gift is given to all, a response is called for. This response is repentance and faith.

Lord

The early Church gave this title to Jesus after the resurrection. By the time Luke writes his Gospel, the title was in common usage. It is not really surprising that Luke, therefore, uses the title of Jesus. It is used in two ways in the Gospel:

1   It is used simply as a word meaning 'sir' or 'master'. When the leper came to Jesus he said,

>   Sir, if only you will, you can cleanse me (5:12).

2   It is used as a word of adoration and praise. The message of the angel to the shepherds at the birth of Jesus was,

>   Today in the city of David, a deliverer has been born to you, the Messiah – the Lord (2:11).

Jesus: Lord for today

This title is still used today by the majority of Christians as a title of adoration. The title expresses the view that Christ's rule is over everything, a rule that will one day be recognised throughout the world.

He is Lord of all creation. They would agree with the earliest statement of belief in Christianity, stretching back to the earliest Church: Jesus is Lord.

SUMMARY

There are three main titles in Luke's Gospel. One is used by Jesus. The other two are used of Jesus in the Gospel narrative.

- Jesus is the Son of Man. He is one who must suffer and die but who will be raised from the dead. He will be given power and will return in Glory to assist in God's judgment and the setting up of God's kingdom on earth.
- Jesus is the Messiah – the Christ, anointed by the spirit of God; chosen for his task to bring all people back to God. This Messiah would suffer and be put to death and rise again.
- Jesus is the Son of God, enjoying a unique relationship with God, his father.

Further to the three main titles, Luke introduces two others that were to become important to both the early Church and the Church of every age.

- Jesus is Saviour, someone who offers freedom from sin and a return to God.
- Jesus is Lord; Lord of all creation.

Study Skills

Knowledge

1 According to Luke, which title did Jesus use to refer to himself?
2 Which Old Testament book talks about the 'Son of Man'?
3 Which Old Testament prophet writes about the Suffering Servant?
4 Give an account of the theme of suffering contained in the sayings of the 'Son of Man' in Luke's Gospel.
5 What do the words Christ/Messiah mean?
6 What did the Jews expect the Messiah to do?
7 In which two stories does God call Jesus his son?
8 On which occasion, in Luke's Gospel is Jesus called deliverer or saviour?
9 In the account of the Temptations, what was Jesus tempted to do?

10 What did John the Baptist preach about the coming of Jesus?

11 What question did the disciples of John the Baptist ask Jesus when John sent them to him?

12 Give an account of the teaching of Jesus in the synagogue at Nazareth.

Understanding

13 At the time of Jesus some Jews held a popular idea of the role of the Messiah. What was this idea? How did Jesus show he was different from their expectation?

14 Explain the importance of the title 'Son of Man' for Jesus. How does Jesus combine this title with the prophecies about the Suffering Servant of Isaiah?

Evaluation

15 What does it mean for Christians today to believe that Jesus was 'the Son of God'?

16 In what ways do you think the title 'Son of Man' is important for Christians today?

Examination Practice

'He stood up to read the lesson and was handed the scroll of the prophet Isaiah. He opened the scroll and found the passage which says,

> "The spirit of the Lord is upon me because he has anointed me;
> he has sent me to announce good news to the poor,
> to proclaim release for prisoners and recovery of sight for the blind;
> to let the broken victims go free.
> to proclaim the year of the Lord's favour."

He rolled up the scroll, gave it back to the attendant, and sat down, and all eyes in the synagogue were fixed on him.

He began to speak: 'Today', he said, 'in your very hearing this text has come true.'

What is the Hebrew word for 'anointed one'?   (1)

What does Jesus mean by saying that the text has come true even as they were listening?   (8)

Name another occasion when Jesus is called either 'God's anointed' or 'his chosen one'   (1)

What do you think is the importance of this story to Luke?   (4)

How important is it for Christians today to believe that Jesus is the anointed one of God?   (6)

Practical Work

- Arrange for one or two representatives or religious leaders such as a Roman Catholic priest, an Anglican priest or a Non-Conformist minister to give a series of short talks and answer questions on the subject of 'Who is Jesus?'

Index of Lukan References